DETAILING & MODIFYING READY-TO-RUN LOCOS IN OO GAUGE

DETAILING & MODIFYING READY-TO-RUN LOCOMOTIVES IN OO GAUGE

VOLUME I

British Diesel & Electric Locomotives, 1955–2008

GEORGE DENT

THE CROWOOD PRESS

First published in 2009 by
The Crowood Press Ltd
Ramsbury, Marlborough
Wiltshire SN8 2HR

www.crowood.com

British Library Cataloguing-in-Publication Data
A catalogue record for this book is available from the British Library.

ISBN 978 1 84797 093 0

Typeset by Servis Filmsetting Ltd, Stockport, Cheshire
Printed and bound in Singapore by Craft Print International Ltd

Contents

Preface and Acknowledgements 6

Introduction 8

1 RESEARCH 11

2 THE TOOLS OF THE TRADE 17

3 GILDING THE LILY 27

4 INTERIOR DESIGN 42

5 A NUMBER OR A NAME 51

6 FIRST STEPS IN CUSTOMIZING 66

7 GOING A LITTLE FURTHER 77

8 COUPLING-UP 89

9 THINK ELECTRIC 101

10 LOOKING UNDERNEATH 109

11 PAINTING 118

12 WEATHERING 129

13 COSMETIC SURGERY 138

14 WHAT MONEY CAN'T BUY 145

15 A NEW SET OF WHEELS 158

16 LIGHT FANTASTIC 167

17 BORN AGAIN? 173

Appendix: Useful Addresses 183

Bibliography 189

Index 191

Preface and Acknowledgements

My first memory of miniature modelling involves being encouraged to build futuristic-looking spacecraft out of empty detergent bottles, cereal boxes and plastic funnels, sating my desire for *Star Wars*-inspired playthings that my parents could not afford. As I got older and was trusted with a craft knife and glue, I eventually progressed to Airfix or matchbox tank and aircraft kits, just like countless other children. In fact, model railways were one of the later disciplines (of those that were open to me) that I tried my hand at, brought about by the gift of a small Lima train set and a couple of Airfix construction kits of OO-gauge cattle-wagons. From here there was no turning back!

These early experiences fostered a habit of thrift and a desire to learn new skills, cementing a mindset that said 'why not just make it myself?' that spread to all manner of things, from building guitars to complete house renovations. I've now been a professional model-maker for nearly a decade, working for museums (most notably at the National Railway Museum in York), businesses and individuals, before joining the team at Model Rail, one of the most popular model railway magazines on the market.

My own interests lie in modelling my namesake station on the scenic Settle–Carlisle line, encompassing the early BR period right through to the present day; although my heart will always be in the early 1980s era, as this was when I spent most of my time watching real trains around North West England. In contrast to this, I'm also in the process of assembling a smaller layout set in Egypt during the Second World War and this has necessitated having to convert or scratch-build virtually every item of motive power and rolling stock.

Apart from the odd digression into O and N gauges, I've always found myself drawn to modelling in OO gauge, despite never really having sufficient space for my desired layouts. However, we all have our foibles and OO has always felt 'right' to me, even if it does have an inherent inaccuracy of track gauge.

ACKNOWLEDGEMENTS

Firstly, I owe a special debt of gratitude to my father for the skills that he patiently sought to encourage in me, along with igniting my imagination and curiosity into all manner of things mechanical and artistic.

Thank you to my colleagues at Model Rail: to Chris Leigh for his support and advice, to Ben Jones for his railway knowledge and to Dave Lowery for his practical hints and tips. I should also mention my appreciation for the many readers who have passed on their ideas and suggestions.

The assistance of Dennis Lovett at Bachmann and Simon Kohler at Hornby in supplying most of the models featured here is much appreciated. Alex Medwell of the Airbrush Company and John Bristow at Deluxe Materials have both been very generous with painting equipment, tools and adhesives. Help from the following has also been very welcome: Charlie Petty (DC Kits), John Peck (Precision Labels), Hurst Models, Chris Gilson and Tony Gadd.

Thanks also to little Maude who came along at the right time to save my sanity, to Pietro for the 'special' coffees that have fuelled the writing of this book and to Bettina and her family for looking after me in Peterborough over the past four years. Final appreciation goes to my wife, Julie-Marie, who enticed me to destroy my television and to embrace life – and hobbies – with real gusto. Life has been much richer since: thank you, Pips. I'd dedicate this book to you but I know you prefer steam-engines . . .

Here's the author toiling away, fuelled by endless cups of tea and inspired by the sound of nearby trains on the Buxton line.

Introduction

Hopefully all modellers, whatever level their skill or experience, will find something helpful in this volume. Techniques will be described and demonstrated within the framework of numerous practical projects. Subsequent chapters will then aim to build on this knowledge, with levels of difficulty increasing as the book progresses. This does not mean that readers can't simply dip into the book to find something to suit their taste, although a little cross-referencing of earlier sections may be necessary. I've endeavoured to include a broad range of subjects here, dealing with a comprehensive list of diesel and electric prototypes, each illustrating a specific skill, method or material.

Diesel and electric traction had been pioneered, to varying extents, before the existence of British Railways (BR). Most notably, the mainline locomotives trialled by both the Southern and the London Midland and Scottish Railways provided invaluable experience. The subtitle of this volume indicates that the period between 1955 and 2008 is our focus; the earlier date denoting the launch of BR's Modernization Plan. Part of this Plan envisaged the end of steam traction and progress in this matter was swift. However, such haste is rarely productive, and the sanctioning of many untested diesel and electric traction designs led to major problems and, coupled with declining traffic levels, left many of these new machines redundant within a decade.

Mainline locomotive construction in Britain ended in the 1990s, when the Brush-built Classes 60 (diesel) and 92 (dual-voltage electric)

entered service. With privatization, foreign-built machines have become the traction of choice for many freight operators, while passenger traffic is almost exclusively in the hands of multiple units. Despite this move to a more standardized railway, there is still much of interest in the contemporary scene and, although modern locomotives may appear bland, closer study can reveal unique details, modifications and livery variations.

As far as the present state of the model railway hobby is concerned, it's tempting to say that we've never had it so good. The standard of today's 'off-the-shelf' products, in detail, accuracy and performance, are of a level way beyond what was available when I was a youngster. The advent of cheaper and more sophisticated manufacturing processes in China has had an enormous impact on the hobby. We can lament the loss of our home-based production and worry about the environmental impact of shipping all our leisure products from across the globe, but the sea change in specification is real and serves to heighten our expectations further and further. This must feel like a double-edged sword for those in charge of Hornby, Bachmann and so on, as, for every new model that hits the shelves, we customers are looking for constant improvements, to the point where even the most minor of detail imperfections can result in a new product receiving a lukewarm or even hostile reception, especially from the press. Happily, this has been quite rare and the constant raising of standards has seen an array of beautiful models over the past decade.

ABOVE: Hornby's brand new version of the Class 56 (left) replaces their previous offering (right) that dates back to the early 1980s. After substantial detailing work, the more mature model still stands up well to its younger brother, but will always be inferior in the mechanical department.

BELOW: A joint venture between Murphy's Models and Bachmann Europe produced this excellent OO-gauge model of CIE's GM-built Class 141/181 Bo-Bo diesel electric locomotives. Despite having an incorrect wheel gauge, the models have proved very popular, stimulating interest in model Irish railways.

Hornby, Lima, Bachmann, Heljan and ViTrains have all produced OO models of the one-time ubiquitous BR/Brush Class 47. This is a Lima model, bought some 15 years ago and with a few hours' worth of detailing work put in.

A more recent development has been the newfound viability of short-run or even one-off prototype locomotives being produced in ready-to-run (r-t-r) form, something that would have been akin to commercial suicide a few years ago. Bachmann's prototype 'Deltic' is an example of this, produced in conjunction with the National Railway Museum. The success of these ventures has now paved the way for other runs of models commissioned by the larger model retailers that would otherwise not be deemed worthwhile for a mass market.

So, is there still anything for modellers to do with the contemporary, high specification OO-gauge r-t-r locomotives? Depending on how realistic you intend your layout to be, there are a number of questions that should be considered: is there a minor detail error or omission? Would you prefer a specific running number or name? Is your favourite livery available? Are you happy for your new locomotives to run with empty cabs?

Does the pristine or factory-weathered finish look good enough? How about that 'oddball' machine with the non-standard headlight arrangement or modified grilles? Many of these issues will not bother many modellers, which is fine. However, some of these points must be addressed in order to get the model you want, rather than what is available to buy.

Naturally, it will take time before manufacturers overhaul their entire range of r-t-r locomotives. Therefore, it's very likely that we will have to entertain the use of some products that may appear a little long in the tooth. Thickly moulded details, over-scale wheels, unsightly couplings and erratic power units leave them seeming almost toy-like against newer offerings. Nevertheless, making convincing improvements to these models is not just for the most dedicated and skilled modellers, but also well within the realms of anyone possessing a little patience, care and willingness to have a go.

CHAPTER 1

Research

Many of us, when starting out in railway modelling, are driven by the desire to capture the essence of a certain moment or place. For me, it was travelling behind a pair of Class 37s between Shrewsbury and Dovey Junction in 1986. The remote landscape and lonely passing loops, plus the curiosity of each protracted station stop (the platforms being far too short to accommodate our train), all combined to leave a sharp imprint on the young mind of someone who had only known local urban train journeys in and around Merseyside.

Even before reaching our destination, I had resolved to build my first 'real' layout based on this route and I eventually settled on a representation of Welshpool, built along a shelf in my tiny bedroom. It was hardly an accurate recreation and the second-hand turnouts were a constant source of frustration, but it did set me along the road of layout construction and rolling stock enhancement. I never felt limited to running a particular range of locomotives or stock, although this was restricted to what I could afford with my pocket money. The odd seasonal gift, however, led to some un-prototypical traction and rolling stock finding its way through my own little bit of mid-Wales, although this didn't bother me unduly at the time. This attitude stays with many of us throughout our modelling 'careers' and, if the hobby still brings enjoyment, then that is all that matters.

However, some feel called towards a higher degree of authenticity and the desire to push the boundaries of what is achievable in a scale model. This may not appeal to everyone, but there must surely be a collective desire for higher levels of detail and accuracy, as this is what appears to drive model manufacturers to strive for continuous improvement in their OO-gauge ranges. I accept that there may be some innovations that are industry-led (such as digital command control; DCC) but, on the whole, this is a consumer-driven business. Otherwise, I'm sure that manufacturers would still be pushing rather basic reproductions onto the market and saving themselves tens of thousands of pounds in research and development costs.

WHEN THE URGE STRIKES

Whether or not you've spent your hard-earned cash on the latest Bachmann Class 37, or are still hanging on to your Lima version, you may soon ask yourself if any improvements could be made. Alternatively, perhaps, it's the realization that a particular locomotive is not (nor is likely to be) available off-the-shelf that has encouraged a desire to start tinkering.

Whatever improvements or modifications you may have envisaged, I wouldn't recommend simply wielding a knife with gay abandon without first doing some research. This will stand you in good stead and, in this modern information age, there are plenty of outlets where an image of an individual locomotive can be found. Knowing where to look is the big secret, and the internet, in particular, has made life much easier; simply typing in the running number of a particular machine into a search engine (such as Google) will usually bring about some interesting results. There are some fantastic websites devoted to single locomotive classes that feature extensive image galleries, technical information, allocation histories and disposal details. *See* the Useful Sources Appendix for some examples.

The web is also home to many enthusiasts' forums and societies, where like-minded people can get in touch and share their knowledge and experience. For those of a non-steam persuasion, DEMU (Diesel and Electric Modellers United) is probably the best port of call for anyone seeking help in this respect. Membership rates are cheap and there is a network of contacts and gatherings around the country, plus regular issues of the society's journal *UPDate*.

There are, of course, plenty of magazine titles catering for the railway modeller, a couple of which concentrate solely on the diesel and electric (D&E) scene. Despite the post-steam era becoming much more popular, the only stand-alone D&E title of recent years, *Modern Railway Modelling* could not sustain a viable readership, even as a quarterly. Other D&E modelling titles are offered as pull-out supplements in *Rail Express* and *Traction* magazines.

For the general market, the 'grandfather' of all model railway magazines is Peco's *Railway Modeller*, a long-standing and largely contribution-based publication that covers anything from 'pre-Grouping' steam to up-to-date subjects. A relatively new entrant is the eye-catching *Hornby Magazine*, produced by Ian Allan and, despite the name, does not concentrate solely on Hornby products. Its key subject area is the early (pre-1980s) BR epoch and the magazine exudes a very nostalgic atmosphere. My own title, *Model Rail*, tries to cover as many areas of railway interest as possible (in all scales) and is largely unique in also incorporating overseas subjects too. Other titles out there include *British Railway Modelling* and the finescale-promoting bi-monthly *Model Railway Journal*. Although I shouldn't be promoting my rivals, all of these magazines are worth browsing through for D&E-related features and some welcome written enquiries by post or email.

If, like me, you've been hoarding magazines for decades but can never remember which issue a particular article appeared in, there are magazine indexes that are freely searchable on the internet. Assembling folders of magazine cuttings can be useful, organizing them by locomotive class and/or period. Untold pleasure can be had from this activity, especially on those long winter evenings (this is what happens when you get rid of your TV!) and it is a real boon when researching a modelling project.

At least 200 new book titles with a railway

Many magazines cater for the model railway market, the majority of which have 4mm scale as their core subject. Some titles lean more towards either the steam/transition era or diesel and electric subjects, while others try to cover as many areas of the hobby as possible. Oh, and there's also the overseas modelling titles!

There are plenty of titles devoted to 'real' trains, some of which specialize in the post-steam era. Up-to-date information can be found within their pages, along with historical essays on particular prototypes.

Copies of old railway magazines are a treasure trove of useful contemporary information and can be picked up cheaply from second-hand book dealers or even junk shops. These issues from the 1960s are packed with details of the 'new' diesels and electrics being introduced on BR.

theme have emerged every year since 1990, a vast increase on the double-figure amounts of the pre-1980 period. There are many reasons for this publishing phenomenon, not least the reduction in production costs of recent years. Needless to say, however, whatever locomotive you may be modelling, it will doubtless have been the subject of several publications. It's worth noting that volumes dealing expressly with a particular locomotive class are not the only books that are of use to the modeller. Indeed, the more generic 'album'-style publications can also throw up lots of useful visual information, perhaps showing a particular engine at just the right time or with an interesting modification not seen elsewhere.

Railway book publishing has exploded in the past few decades and there are plenty of volumes from which to gain inspiration. Profile-type books are very useful for technical information, while the more generic album-style is also helpful.

Armed with magazine cuttings and a range of books and photographs, the keen detailer is well equipped to produce an accurate model of a chosen prototype.

It helps to have a friend who owns a real locomotive! Many preservation societies are receptive to courteous modellers and there are plenty of open days in the calendar too. This is 47492 undergoing restoration.

Dedicated railway and transport bookshops are to be found all over Britain, many of which offer mail order and internet-based shopping. Such outlets often specialize in second-hand or out-of-print volumes, and some can also track down copies of specific works for you. Publishers, such as Ian Allan and Midland Counties, also offer a direct shopping service. An often-overlooked source of information is your local authority's public library, whose catalogue will probably be searchable online. If they don't have the title you're after, then making use of the inter-library loans system enables copies of specific books to be borrowed from other libraries for only a small charge. The library and archive at the National Railway Museum has recently undergone a radical overhaul and their collections are now much more accessible; they don't just have boxes of historic drawings and documents, but also an excellent range of reference books, magazines and journals.

SUBJECTS 'IN THE FLESH'

Despite the plethora of printed material out there, sometimes there is no substitute for actually getting out and studying the real thing. However, this is not always appropriate, especially if your prototype no longer exists. The increased popularity of 'diesel gala' days at preserved railways can afford the opportunity of photographing certain classes in action. Remember, though, that preserved machines are not always in fully 'authentic' condition, commensurate with their heritage liveries or physical appearance.

Modellers of the contemporary scene obviously have things a little easier, as they can get out and photograph their chosen subjects. As most locomotives are now only to be found working freight services, a copy of the latest *Freightmaster* timetable is an essential companion. Magazines such as *Rail* and *Rail Express* can also keep you abreast of current traffic flows and locomotive allocations. Other helpful outlets are also the websites of the train-operating companies themselves, many of which have enthusiast-friendly pages dealing with liveries and traction information.

If you feel the need to get closer to the object of your obsession, then most preservation societies are approachable and a polite request can often be met with an invitation to have a look around a locomotive, sometimes in return for some voluntary work or a donation to the group's coffers. However you get to see a real locomotive, it will help to capture enough images and, if necessary, take appropriate measurements in order to help with your modelling. Some example images are included here, of a Class 27 parked at Lydney Junction on the Dean Forest Railway, to illustrate the sort of areas to which attention should be paid. Obviously, some shots of the roof would have been handy, but these are often the most difficult images to obtain. A little tip is to engage the assistance of someone with, say, a metre rule and to have he/she hold it in each picture near to the area in question. This way, in the comfort of your home, fairly accurate dimensions can be ascertained from the photographs, scaling them appropriately.

An array of hoses, pipes and jumper cables adorn the front of locomotives, each colour-coded according to use. Note also the lifeguards in front of the leading wheels.

Look at the footsteps above the buffer, fabricated from chequer plate steel. There's also another tread step atop the buffer shank with 'OLEO' cast into it.

Fuel tanks and battery boxes, slung beneath the chassis, usually contain runs of pipework and conduit not featured on most production-scale models. Filling points, gauge dials and drain cocks are all visible here.

Although this is a well-maintained machine, notice the streaks running hither and thither, as well as the odd patch of rust and chipped paint, particularly beneath the cab door.

MAKING A START

Many of my modelling projects have begun life after chancing upon a particular photograph in a magazine or book; an image that happens to include plenty of pertinent detail features or livery variations. When producing an accurate, era-specific model for the first time, I'd certainly recommend using such a shortcut instead of choosing a particular locomotive and then trying to find the right information. Research is a skill that is acquired and honed over time, just as the practical techniques of modelling are. The more you do it, the easier it will be to identify the right sources and filter out extraneous information.

And so, armed with enough information (or as much as can be found), we can set forth on to the practical side. However, before hurtling head-on into this, some discussion of materials, tools and techniques is necessary.

CHAPTER 2

The Tools of the Trade

'A craftsman is only as good as the tools he uses' is an oft-repeated phrase, although I'm not sure if this is more of a sales pitch from tool manufacturers than a true reflection of a craftsperson's skill. I studied wood-carving and cabinet-making for a number of years, and virtually all of the experienced craftsmen that I met had long since streamlined their tool chests to a minimum of well-trusted implements. Not only was this down to jobbing carvers being unwilling to be laden with boxes of chisels of every size and shape, but also due to feeling comfortable and familiar with a specific set and, more importantly, having confidence in their own ability.

This is equally true of the experienced model-maker who may experiment with many of the tools and devices on the market but will probably, for most undertakings, stick to what has served well in the past. A good number of items in my 'front line' tool-kit were passed on from my father, so must date back quite a few years!

More specialist tools have their place and I've been lucky to receive various gadgets and implements as review samples through *Model Rail* magazine. Some have been better than others and, without naming names, those that are collecting dust somewhere in the shed have not managed to 'make the cut', while a select few (well, half a dozen or so) are kept at hand for specific tasks, but more of these later.

ASSEMBLING A TOOL-KIT

As I spend a fair amount of time travelling down to my magazine's HQ, I thought it a good idea to develop a duplicate tool-set. This allows me to have some familiar implements at hand when I'm in the office and, due to its 'mobile' nature, also keeps me out of mischief while staying away from home. Moreover, this mobile set epitomizes the 'less is more' facet of working, as most of the tools required for many of the projects

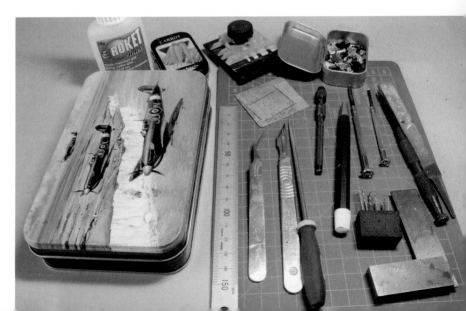

So many detailing projects can be undertaken with the minimum of equipment. This is my 'mobile' kit, which includes some basic measuring, marking and cutting tools, plus drills, files, tweezers and pliers. The small seed tins are perfect for holding drill bits and detailing components. An A5 cutting mat and a couple of essential adhesives complete the set.

contained in this book are cheap to buy and will happily fit inside a small tin.

There's no doubt that some 'luxury' items can make a huge impact in terms of saving time and ensuring consistent, professional-looking results and, in particular, it's worth paying a little more for measuring, marking and cutting tools. Other items that are just as essential are a self-healing cutting mat, a decent vice and a good lamp. Also, I can't overstate the benefits of having a good-quality soldering iron, even if only used for repairing electrical connections. Putting an inferior heat tool anywhere near an expensive and delicate model seems foolish and invariably proves a false economy. I've gone through a number of 'cheapo' irons in my time and the frustration that such things cause can be avoided by spending a little more in the first place.

For the projects outlined in this book, there are a number of instances where the use of a soldering iron would be beneficial, although if you're not entirely confident in this process just yet, then glue can be substituted. Choosing the right soldering iron, flux and solder for each job is important, and it's rare, save for in the construction of etched brass locomotive kits,

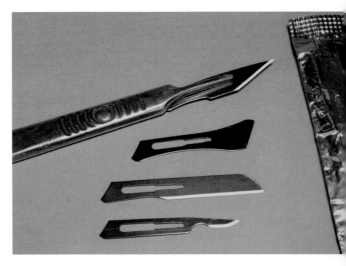

Most hobby and craft knives come in the form of a separate handle with interchangeable blades. Be sure to change the blade regularly to prevent damaging the model or causing accidents.

for a soldering iron of more than 12–18watts in power to be required. Some iron manufacturers provide for interchangeable bits, of varying sizes and shapes, to suit specific tasks. Temperature controlled tools are also available, some with digital temperature readouts and these, although expensive, provide great flexibility.

It goes without saying that the need for care (both towards your person and the model in question) is paramount. Get yourself a decent iron stand and, if possible, a heat-resistant pad on which to work. Inhaling the fumes emitted from molten solder and evaporating flux is in no way good for the lungs and should be avoided as much as possible; work in a well-ventilated room and wash your hands thoroughly afterwards.

Another note of caution must be stated with regard to the use of sharp implements. Sharp is the operative word here, as a blunt tool should never be used anywhere near a model. Not only will a dull blade, drill, scriber or scraper make a mess of the work-piece but it's also just as dangerous (if not more so) than a razor sharp

A handy and economical way of increasing the versatility of your soldering iron is to replace the main's plug with a temperature regulator, such as this unit from the Antex range. Although a read-out of iron bit temperature is not offered, a bit of trial and error makes it an easy tool to master.

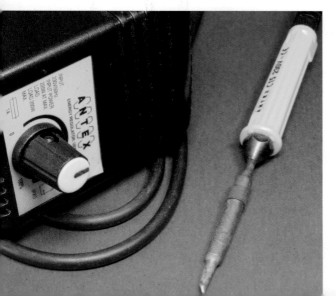

tool. Exerting pressure on a blunt tool will result in loss of control and I have the scars to prove a number of mishaps, when I should have just swapped the blade and let the tool do the work. As will be reiterated a number of times throughout this book, if cutting away any amount of plastic with a knife, always work gradually, taking just a slither at a time; this will leave a better finish, prolong the life of the cutting edge and possibly avoid a trip to A&E.

For light-to-medium duty tasks, I've been using the same scalpel since my college days: a Swann Morton No.3 handle along with various blade patterns, such as Nos 9, 10, 11A and 15C. For tougher or thicker materials, the 'old faithful' Stanley knife is used, as well as an X-Acto No.5 knife handle with a selection of heavy duty blades that can work into narrower corners than the standard Stanley blade.

Marking-out with a single-edged blade or scribing tool is a sure way to achieving a high degree of accuracy in all materials. The width of a pencil line can mean the difference of nearly three inches in 4mm scale.

Other 'edged' tools that come in handy are miniature centre punches and scribers. Punches prevent drill bits from wandering away from the exact location that they should be cutting through, as well as punching-out rivets on some etched detailing components. Scribers, if kept absolutely sharp, are perfect for marking-out brass and plastic components, as well as adding missing panel seams and so on. Such tools need sharpening regularly, using either a bench grinder or an oilstone.

Another useful tip, which I picked up while studying cabinet-making, involves the use of a single-edged knife blade for marking-out plastic components. This is a much more accurate method than using a pencil and ruler, as the width of the pencil line (which can be anything from 0.5 to 1.5mm-thick) actually interferes with the final dimensions. A good way of demonstrating this is to draw two lines, measured 20mm apart. Now take another look at your two lines and work out at which point they are exactly 20mm apart: on the outside edges of the pencil strokes, the centre, or the inside? Now use a single-edged blade, the flat edge held against the ruler, and mark two more identical lines. The exact 20mm-distance is between the two cut edges and, therefore, you have a perfectly sized component. Depending on the material in question, the marked lines can either be used as a guide for another blade or saw to cut toward, or the marking knife can simply cut through the whole thing.

On the topic of measuring, a set of digital callipers are certainly a justified investment, being much easier to use than the traditional Vernier type. The convenience of a digital readout and instant metric–imperial conversion is very welcome, especially when dealing in measurements of thousands of an inch. As part of a generation brought up on the metric system, fractions of an inch still leave me somewhat perplexed, not helped by many modelling materials and products being sold in imperial units. Having a little machine to do the maths saves a lot of brain ache and the price of these tools has fallen considerably in recent years. My own set is OK for my needs, although they do have an annoying habit of eating-up batteries rather too quickly. I suppose you get what you pay for and, for £20, I can't really complain.

As will be seen through the following chapters, drills and bits play an essential role in even the most basic of detailing undertakings. Indeed, even adding the brake hoses supplied with new model locomotives will often require the moulded holes to be opened-out slightly to accept them. Miniature twist-drill bits are cheap and readily available and it's worth keeping a few spares of the most popular sizes (say 0.4, 0.5, 0.7, 0.9 and 1mm diameter) as they are liable to break at the most inopportune moment, especially if used in an electric mini-drill. Moreover, I'd advise against using a power drill when cutting a hole less than 1mm in size, as it will invariably lead to either a broken bit or, worse, the heat build-up will cause the plastic to melt and result in an over-sized hole. Instead, be a little more patient and use a needle vice and cut your holes by hand. This keeps you entirely in control of the tool and less likely to make mistakes.

It's interesting to browse through modelling magazines from different disciplines, as some techniques or new products, although designed with, for example, the aircraft modeller in mind, will potentially prove invaluable to railway modellers. Military modellers seem to be an especially proactive bunch, as far as tool-making is concerned, and a number of devices have recently made the cross-over into the railway field, most notably with Cammett UK's 'Hold 'n' Fold' and 'Nutter' devices. These can be best described as quality miniature engineering tools and, although not cheap, they soon prove their usefulness. The purpose of the 'Hold 'n' Fold' is self-explanatory, and is unbeatable for producing accurate shapes in sheet metal, as well as doubling as a hand vice to aid construction of small assemblies. Available in a range of sizes to suit various tasks, the 4mm-scale modeller would be advised to look at the small and/or medium size (2in or 6in) tools that are suitable for various applications, as will be demonstrated later. The 'Nutter' is another very useful device that allows for individual rivets, bolts and nuts to be stamped from thin foil, in different sizes. This is perfect for detailing and modification work, where new panels need to be fixed in place. It can often prove more economical to make your own detailing components, as well as offering the chance to produce more

When accuracy is required, forego the mini power-drill and use the old-fashioned pin vice to retain complete control over the tool. A decent set of bits, in 0.5mm increments, is not an expensive purchase, although keeping a few spares of the most popular sizes is a good idea.

Purpose-built tools, such as Cammett's 'Hold 'n' Fold' and 'Nutter', are designed and built by modellers for modellers. Professional-looking and consistent results are obtainable using such devices and they soon pay for themselves in terms of time saved.

The essentials of successful modelling: a steady work surface, cutting mat, basic tool set, adhesives, good lighting, power points and a vice. Daylight simulating lamps help enormously, especially when matching colour shades. In reality, my desk is not always so tidy but an uncluttered workspace is a safer one.

accurate parts than those otherwise available, and both the 'Nutter' and 'Hold 'n' Fold' will prove invaluable in this respect.

Along with the correct tools, the other crucial requirement for successful and enjoyable model-making is a suitable space; preferably with the benefit of good natural and/or artificial light, ventilation and free from interference from spouses, small offspring and exuberant animals. A large amount of space is not essential but a stable work-surface is. As most modellers will testify, many components end up disappearing into the wilderness of a carpet, so why not try having a small, light-coloured piece of linoleum or a shallow-pile rug beneath the workbench to make it easier to find that errant lamp bracket or wiper. Mind you, I've found that it's usually quicker to just bite my tongue and make another part rather than spend thirty minutes on hand and knees scouring the floor!

Adequate lighting is paramount to maintain the optimum performance of your eyeballs and,

while desktop spotlight lamps are sufficient, try fitting daylight-simulating bulbs, which emit a softer, cooler kind of light. These are invaluable for colour matching, as regular bulbs alter our perception of shades markedly.

MATERIALS

As we're dealing with ready-to-run models, the most common material that we'll encounter is plastic. In most instances, locomotive bodyshells are injection-moulded using a polystyrene-based compound, while bogie frames and chassis units are usually formed of a harder, self-coloured and oil-resistant material, such as ABS (Acrylonitrile Butadiene Styrene – the same thermoplastic as used in Lego bricks). Both have their own distinct properties that lend themselves to their own application but also determine how (and with what tools) we work with them.

As Chapter 10 will testify, there is much to be done below platform level on some models and we need to be aware that different materials will behave somewhat, well, differently. I'll talk about adhesives in the following chapter but, as far as tools are concerned, don't expect even the sharpest knife to cut through a bogie frame as easily as it would through a moulded cab handrail. Take great care and remove a little plastic at a time. Additionally, if more than a few millimetres of this tough material are to be removed, don't be tempted to try and hack it away with a knife. Instead use a razor saw or (if you're confident enough) a slitting disc in a mini power drill, cutting just shy of the final size and working back with a file and abrasive paper to achieve a neat and accurate finish.

Most good model shops will stock a range of plastic card, strip, section and rod, usually from the Evergreen or Slaters ranges, and these are produced in a wide variety of sizes. Having a stock of these to hand is always helpful when scratchbuiding new components, such as door hinges, window blinds or underframe equipment. Plastic does have its limits, however, most notably in its lack of inherent rigidity when

formed into thin section. Thus, many locomotive models are supplied with separate handrails, lamp brackets and windscreen wipers that are well over-scale but impossible to produce in finer relief without them simply disintegrating upon human contact. Some of the more recent high-specification offerings are now complete with etched brass components or wire handrails, but this is far from becoming standard equipment.

Therefore, most of the parts that we will be adding to our models will be in the form of either brass or nickel silver etches or white-metal castings. White-metal is an alloy that usually contains a large proportion of lead and (donning my health and safety hat again) can be detrimental to one's health if care is not taken in handling and working with it. Always wash your hands after touching any components, especially before eating, and keep it away from the kids. Some makers of detailing parts are now substituting lead-free pewter which is much more attractive as it tends to take a finer degree of detail, depending on the quality of the mould.

Photo-etched (or just 'etched' in modellers'

Most model shops should hold a stock of plastic sheet, section, strip and rod, a huge range of sizes being available, they provide a very cheap way to scratchbuild components.

Brass and copper sheet, section, tube and wire are also essential materials. Craft stores sell various gauges of steel, brass or nickel silver wire aimed at jewellery making, which is very economically priced.

There's a bewildering amount of etched or cast detailing components available for virtually every r-t-r (and some kit-built) diesel or electric locomotive models. The ranges of A1 Models and Shawplan are perhaps the best-known and include packs of single components or complete detailing or conversion kits.

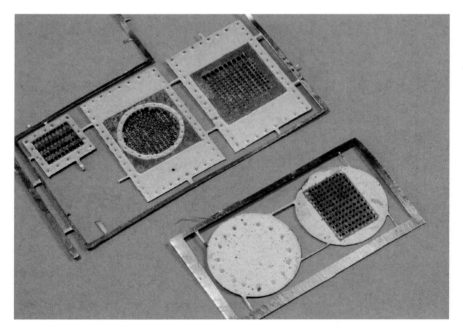

Many component packs offer alternative parts to cover variations in locomotive equipment. For instance, these A1 Models Class 47 boiler ports include each of the patterns with which the class were fitted.

Polyurethane resin has its pros and cons but, when applied sensibly, it is a very useful medium. These bogie frames are from a DC Kits AC electric locomotive kit, while the bodyshell is from a Scotrail Mark2 DBSO kit.

shorthand) metal components make up the majority of detailing parts available off-the-shelf. Brass is the most common material employed for this process and is a pleasing metal to work with. It can also be formed into the most delicate of patterns without losing its natural strength. Nickel silver (and, to a lesser degree, stainless steel) is also a popular medium for applications where inflexibility is paramount, such as nameplates or complex flat-grille arrangements. Aside from etched parts, brass is also available in various gauges of stiff or flexible wire from which handrails, pipes, conduit and hoses can all be fashioned quickly and easily. Steel guitar strings and fishing line are also very useful for various applications.

Another material that is gaining popularity in railway modelling is polyurethane resin. This is a soft and brittle compound, although it will take a good amount of detail from a well-made mould. Hence, resin components are usually cast in thick section to prevent breakage and are there-fore limited in their application to bogie frames and one-piece bodyshells or underframes.

A pitfall of using resin is its potential threat to a modeller's health. When drilling, filing or sawing this stuff, a very fine but noxious powder is produced. Ensure that a suitable face mask is worn to protect your lungs, and clean your hands afterwards. Another point to bear in mind is that the production process includes the use of a chemical-releasing agent to prevent the resin sticking to the mould. This tends to leave a greasy coating on the components that, unless washed thoroughly with a detergent, will prevent any primer or paint from adhering. Use a cleaner such as 'Cif' and avoid anything like washing-up liquid, as this will only leave another residue.

So, with our tool-kits and workspaces ready, and our appreciation for safety and material suitability in place, we're all set for the 'off'. The following couple of chapters will aim to break-in the novice gently with some rudimentary, but nonetheless worthwhile, projects and tips.

Glues and Gluing

The range of superglues produced by Deluxe Materials is comprehensive and each formula is tailored to specific materials and applications. Accelerating and de-bonding agents are also available, along with various micro-tip applicators to permit neat work in very tight corners.

The Vi-Trains' range of Class 37s requires the supplied wipers to be glued directly to the bodyshell, without any mounting holes provided. Fixing the wipers with odourless superglue will prevent 'blooming' of the glazing.

There's an almost overwhelming array of adhesives on the market these days, all boasting their own specific properties. It's helpful to have a selection of glues at hand for specific tasks, along with suitable applicators, accelerants and, in case of calamity, de-bonding agents. An understanding of each formula's properties and potential is also valuable.

By far the most useful adhesive in model-making is cyanoacrylate – better known as superglue – as it will bond more or less anything to everything, usually within a few seconds. Various viscosities are formulated, each tailored to different situations and, in general, the thicker the liquid, the longer the drying time. This is important as, for example, we may want a little time to adjust the fit of a part before the bond becomes permanent. Conversely, we may not

be able to hold a component in place while it sets, so an instant union is desired. Having a few jars of different types, then, is certainly advantageous.

It should be noted that using superglues in close proximity to clear plastic carries a risk of 'blooming', brought about by evaporating solvent fumes depositing a white residue. If addressed quickly, it can sometimes be removed by rubbing with a dry cotton bud although, more often than not, the damage is permanent. Similar damage to the model's paintwork can also take place if insufficient time is allowed for the solvent to disperse before the locomotive is placed back into its box, the fumes concentrating and damaging the finish, often irrevocably. A way around these problems is to employ an odourless formula, such as that offered by Deluxe Materials.

Mixing two-part epoxy glues can get a bit tedious, but this dual-action dispenser makes life easier. For reliable joints, the same amount of each compound should be used. Epoxies are available in a range of curing times to suit different applications.

The slower curing time of epoxy glue will often require the parts to be clamped in position. Using a quicker-setting formula can cause problems on larger jobs as the adhesive may go 'off' before you've had time to assemble and clamp everything.

Plastic solvents, such as Plastic Magic, act by 'welding' the two plastic surfaces together. This may not be as swift a bond as with superglues but, once set, a very resilient joint is achieved. Needle-point applicators, such as this 'Pin Flow' tool, help to keep the thin liquid under control.

Twin-pack epoxy glues are also manufactured to various specifications to provide a range of setting times. Equal amounts of both liquids need to be mixed thoroughly before application and setting times can be anything from a couple of minutes to an hour. Epoxy will fix most materials and, once thoroughly hardened, provide a more durable bond than superglue, as it retains a degree of flexibility even when set.

I rarely use epoxy glue for adding fine details, as this type of glue has a thick consistency and can be a bit messy. This is fine for most general jobs, where any excess can be wiped away with a damp cloth or cotton bud, but not for fixing tiny lamp brackets or wipers, where the faintest drop of cyanoacrylate will do the trick much better.

For plastic-to-plastic applications, liquid cement is often the best choice. Products such as

Heljan's OO-gauge Classes 26, 27 and 33 all allow for the bufferbeams to be prized away from the chassis after removing the bodyshell; a very convenient feature that reduces the risk of damaging the rest of the model while working. As with most models, the mounting holes need opening-out to accept the brake hoses and this goes for the snowplough brackets too; all can be fixed using a plastic solvent such as Plastic Magic.

Humbrol's Poly Cement, Deluxe's Plastic Magic or Slater's Plastic Weld are all very good in their own way and are each well-suited to various types of plastic. These cements act to soften both plastic components and 'weld' them together at the mating face. Parts can usually be handled within a few minutes but often require an overnight period to harden entirely. Take great care not to use too much liquid cement as, obviously, you'll soften too much plastic; paint finishes are especially susceptible to these solvents.

Other types of adhesives are also of use to us, such as PVA-based glues aimed at fixing glazing or lighting panels and that set absolutely clear. Card and paper glues are beneficial, especially when detailing cab interiors, and for awkward materials such as oily chassis parts, Deluxe's Super Crylic will fix just about anything.

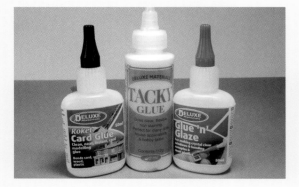

Paper and card glues (fast and slow acting), thick 'tacky' adhesives, and ultra-clear formulas for glazing all have a use in locomotive detailing.

Some materials can be frustratingly difficult to fix together, but Deluxe's Super Crylic two-part adhesive will bond just about anything.

CHAPTER 3

Gilding the Lily

I've already remarked how the standard of r-t-r models has been raised exponentially over the past decade, yet there is still the odd enhancement that can be practiced on even the cream of the recent OO gauge crop. Moreover, as many models now come packaged in an almost-finished state, it is left to the customer to add the few final flourishes, thus providing a window of opportunity to develop our skills.

Packs of bufferbeam-mounted pipes and hoses, windscreen wipers, air horns and, in some cases, etched nameplates are supplied with a model. Bufferbeam parts, in particular, are left as separate fittings as the amount of detail that can be accommodated is dependant upon the type of coupling used. Some of these 'goody bags' contain beautiful little creations, while others, frankly, are a bit of a let down and can actually spoil a model. In other instances, factory-fitted items, such as wipers, may be rather crude plastic mouldings, a case in point being the limited-edition 'Deltic' prototype released by Bachmann in early 2008. This is a fantastic model but is marred slightly by the coarsely moulded wipers and air horns. It's surprising how such small details can leap out, even when viewed from the usual exhibition spectator's distance.

The window of opportunity alluded to above allows some scope for minor customization on virtually all models. It's interesting to note how a more discerning eye can develop, almost unwittingly, once a few detailing projects have been tried. Take a look at any of your latest models and consider where a little improvement can be made. Just a few seemingly tiny tweaks here and there add up to more than you'd think, especially once a bit of careful weathering has been applied. You'll soon realize that for the sake of a few extra pounds and an hour or two's work, a major improvement can be effected. Whatever first steps you take, a number of key techniques will be experienced, namely: measuring, marking, drilling, cutting, filing and a little painting. Various plastics and metals will be encountered and a range of adhesives explored. These are simple but important skills to master and are the first steps along the road to super-detailing. My old carving teacher often pronounced that anyone could carve if they only set their mind to it. It just took time to learn and to develop one's own style and technique. Practice makes perfect, as they say, and I thoroughly agree. Just have a go and don't give up too easily.

BUFFERBEAM EQUIPMENT

This is probably the best place to start, provided of course that your choice of couplings permit adding anything like a full compliment of bufferbeam pipes and hoses. If not, what about fitting them to one end only and keeping the other end for the serious business of stock compatibility? Aside from, maybe, a small exploded diagram within the model's maintenance instructions, roughly illustrating the location of the afforded detailing parts, there is often no mention of the best way to go about fixing them in place. Incidentally, the instructions supplied with Vi-Trains' Class 37 models are by far the best, yet other products contain no mention of part locations.

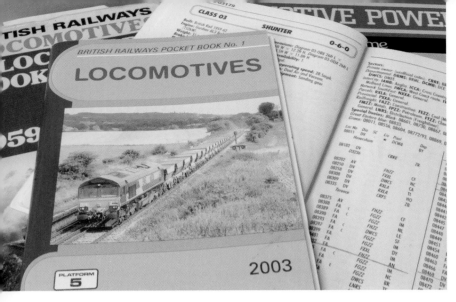

A good source of information is contemporary 'ABC' spotter's books. As my intention was to model 08402, sometime around the 1990 period, I looked up the number in my 1989 'ABC' and noted that it was air brake-only fitted, so added the brake pipes accordingly.

This may sound like stating the obvious, after all how hard can gluing a few bits of plastic in place be? Nevertheless, as I can vouch from the numerous queries that I regularly receive through the 'Q&A' pages of *Model Rail*, it isn't always easy. Commonly, the moulded receiving holes may have been constricted by paint (or not cast big enough in the first place) and require opening-out slightly with a small twist drill, while some components may have no locations provided at all. The type of glue utilized is also important, as is the application method, to avoid damaging the paint finish or causing 'misting' of the clear glazing.

Hornby's little bag of detailing 'goodies' is amongst the best available, even challenging those from the after-market component makers. Choose the right size of drill to suit the mounting lug of the pipe, hose or coupling, using a pair of callipers or a ruler. A drill bit just slightly larger should be used, i.e. for a 1.3mm diameter hose, drill-out the bufferbeam to 1.4mm.

Beginning with one of my favourite recent OO locomotive releases, the Hornby Class 08, the exquisite set of brake pipes and hoses that are supplied require a deceiving amount of care to fit properly. As they're moulded from a very flexible material, they can withstand a few knocks here and there and, more importantly, will not stand in the way of fitting the supplied tension lock-style couplings; something that is much more difficult to do on a model with bogies as the coupling will not be able to swing around curves.

Before adding the brake pipes to any model, do a little research to ascertain whether or not this specific prototype was fitted with either vacuum-only, dual (air and vacuum) brakes or air-only brake equipment in the time period that

To avoid making a mess, decant a blob of superglue on to some scrap card and use a cocktail stick to apply a small amount of glue on to the hose. Push the component into place, ensuring it sits vertically, and hold it for a few seconds until the glue 'grabs'.

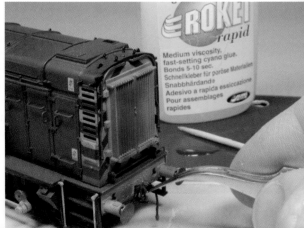

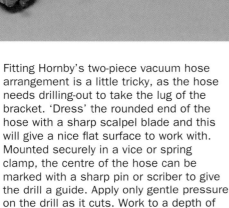

Fitting Hornby's two-piece vacuum hose arrangement is a little tricky, as the hose needs drilling-out to take the lug of the bracket. 'Dress' the rounded end of the hose with a sharp scalpel blade and this will give a nice flat surface to work with. Mounted securely in a vice or spring clamp, the centre of the hose can be marked with a sharp pin or scriber to give the drill a guide. Apply only gentle pressure on the drill as it cuts. Work to a depth of around 3mm to give enough surface area for the glue joint.

Test for a good fit and then fix the pipe bracket in place on the bufferbeam. Once the glue has set, add a tiny drop on to the lug and fix the brake hose, ensuring that it hangs vertically.

you intend to portray, as this will dictate which components are necessary. Further to the sources mentioned in Chapter 1, old copies of 'ABC'-type spotter's books are an excellent source of information and can be picked up in second-hand transport book shops or at exhibitions and swap-meets (or on Ebay), although older issues can command rather high prices. Not all such books have these sorts of technical specifications listed, seemingly being a more post-1980s thing, but the Railway Travel and Correspondence Society (RCTS) has been publishing highly detailed annual BR locomotive registers for decades, and these, again, can be obtained fairly easily.

It can be tempting to try and push the plastic parts straight into their intended holes using a pair of tweezers or long-nose pliers and, some-times, a nice friction fit can be achieved negating the need for adhesives. However, this is the exception and, more often than not, exerting just a little too much pressure will see the hose bending, snapping or catapulting across the full length of the room, never to be seen again. It's a far safer bet to open the hole to a slightly

larger diameter than the locating peg and then, after applying a tiny drop of superglue, pushing the part into place and supporting it for a few seconds while the glue sets. The same applies to the dummy screw couplings.

Depending on the model, Hornby's vacuum brake pipes may come as two-piece mouldings, consisting of a black 'rubber' hose and a small white pipe arrangement that sits below the buff-erbeam and acts as a mounting bracket. This combination is not suitable for every prototype but, if utilized, looks excellent. It is, though, not that easy to assemble, as the end of the hose needs to be drilled-out to accept the lug of the mounting pipe.

In the event of the model's instructions not being clear vis-à-vis locations, then be sure to check prototype photographs to verify that the right pipes and hoses go in the right place and, if necessary, paint the cocks and unions red, yellow, white or orange, as appropriate. These colours are important and denote the purpose of each hose:

- red: air-brake main pipe;
- yellow and white: air-control reservoir pipes;
- orange: electrical connections, such as multi-ple working and train heat;
- silver: steam heat.

Vacuum brake pipes were not allotted a specific colour.

WIPERS, HORNS
AND OTHER STORIES

Where other fine details, such as windscreen wipers or rooftop air horns, do not come factory-fitted, then follow the same procedure of measuring the mounting lugs and drilling-out the holes to permit a nice gentle fit, reinforcing with a tiny blob of glue. A pilot hole is not always supplied, however, and, in the case of the Vi-Trains' Class 37, the pre-painted brass wipers need to be carefully fixed to the top of the bonnets with superglue. It takes but one look at a real '37' to appreciate that the wipers are of a much more delicate and complex pattern than that intimated by Vi-Trains' supplied parts. They're also rather small in comparison to the size of the window aperture; the driver being afforded only a modest area of un-obscured vision in the event of a downpour.

Adding replacement wipers (in pattern and scale) is simplicity itself, a whole range of types being available from detailing component makers. Etched brass offerings in the Craftsman,

A1 Models and Shawplan (amongst others) produce various sizes and patterns of wipers, some packs providing enough parts for a couple of locomotives. It makes life much easier to prime and paint them before fitting.

A1 and Shawplan ranges are complimented by some attractive plastic units obtainable as Class 26, 27 and 33 spares from Heljan. Choose your alternative parts carefully, as locomotives carried various patterns depending on class and period. Repairs and refurbishment also led to a mix of styles, even on a single machine. Removing factory-fitted wipers may just involve pulling them out with a pair of tweezers. If they're glued fast, however, use a sharp blade to slice the 'elbow' away, leaving the lug sitting flush with the surface. A new hole can then be drilled.

Etched wipers can be very delicate parts and require gentle handling. It's better to paint them while still attached to the fret with a quick blast of aerosol primer – the acrylic stuff sold in automotive stores like Halfords is ideal. Follow with a topcoat of black acrylic or enamel, air- or hand-brushed. Most wipers should be matt black, although some early BR types sported polished metal wiper arms, or at least they did when the engines were new. It invariably didn't take long before they turned to a dull grey, while, in any case, the actual blade would always be black rubber.

After colouring, cut one part away from the fret at a time, preferably working on a piece of hardboard. A solid surface such as this will prevent the delicate brass from bending under the knife, as will happen if using a rubber cutting mat, while the wood board will also preserve the life of the blade. Most etched wipers incorporate a mounting lug, which needs to be folded to a right angle from the main arm. Grip near the 'elbow' with a pair of smooth-nose pliers, and fold over the lug using light finger pressure. If no mounting holes already exist, mark out the locations at each window and lightly press a sharp scriber point to create a guide 'pip' to help the drill bit to start its cut.

Care must be used when drilling near to a window, as there's sure to be part of the glazing on the other side of the bodywork through which your drill is cutting; exert too much pressure and the glazing may be dislodged. If you are working without separating the body from the chassis, drilling all the way through the bodyshell may

Most replacement wipers incorporate a fixing lug and a locating hole must be drilled before fitting. The model may already have holes moulded into the bodyshell, but these will require opening-out a tad.

Test fit the wipers first before adding a tiny drop of odourless superglue on to the lug. Push gently into place and make sure the wiper blade sits flush on the surface of the window, just like the prototype.

trap some unsightly waste material inside the cabs. A cure for this is either to dismantle the model or to drill but a shallow hole, cutting the wiper's lug to fit; this shouldn't overly weaken the glue joint.

If mounting holes are already extant, they may need enlarging or, indeed, may be too large. In this event, you have a choice of how to proceed, either by plugging the over-large holes with a model filler, allowing it to harden and then re-drilling to the right size, or otherwise just glue the wipers in place before filling the remaining gaps, using a cocktail stick to push the filler into any tight spots. A little dab of the right shade of paint and 'Bob's your uncle': job done.

Nose or roof-mounted air horns are another very minor feature that can have a disproportionate visual effect on a model. Renewal is not always necessary, as some original fitments can be salvaged, particularly the roof 'hooters' on the Bachmann '37'. The pronounced moulding seam is easy to cut and file away, leaving a nice smooth, rounded profile, utilizing some tiny strips of 400–1,000grade wet or dry abrasive paper. The business end of the horns will benefit from being trimmed to a truly straight and vertical edge, while then proceeding to create a realistic concave profile using a 1.5mm drill bit.

If this task doesn't appeal, then fitting some new horns is the answer and there's a choice of

cast white metal or turned brass replacements available, although some packs only offer four horns of the same length; not strictly accurate for most forms of traction. Longer and shorter 'hooters' each provide their own part of the distinctive 'nee-nor' sound and a set of cast horns are much easier to trim to size than brass turnings.

Instead of replacing a factory-fitted set of air horns, try and refine the mouldings by cutting or filing away any seam lines and cut the bulbous ends straight and vertical. Mark the centre and lightly drill-out the ends to form a concave shape.

If replacements are necessary, pull or cut away the originals and fix a set of cast white metal or turned brass substitutes, putting the long and short horns the right way around. If the castings require trimming, break the horn just in front of the mount, trim that end of the horn and glue both in place. Any small gap can be disguised with a tiny bit of filler.

ETCHED COMPONENTS

Locomotives have carried nameplates and other cast crests and emblems from near the beginning of the railways and are, therefore, important features to include on OO-gauge models. The vast majority of r-t-r offerings are produced with printed nameplates or logotypes plus, maybe, a pack of separate etched replacements supplied should the customer wish to fit them. Modern production methods have permitted these 'flat' representations to look much better than they used to, the 'tampo' printing method allowing a level of paint to be built-up that stands proud of the bodywork, giving a hint of relief.

You can't beat a well-made set of etched components, however, and these are relatively cheap and easy to fit, the main trick being in cutting them cleanly from the fretwork, tidying up the edges and sticking them on straight without making a mess. Another advantage is the use of authentic materials, something that is hard to capture with shades of paint. For polished alloy crests, names and logos, why not simply use stainless steel in its natural form? You can't

get any more accurate-looking than that! A useful example is the distinctive Channel Tunnel logo introduced by BR's Railfreight Distribution sector during the early 1990s. Commonly referred to as 'Polo mints' or 'hoops', the diminishing series of alloy circles is an interesting graphic device and, although Hornby have made a good fist of printing them on their Class 92 models, some etched stainless steel replacements do make a difference.

A pack of Shawplan 'hoops' has been fitted to the Class 92 featured here, although Hurst Models also offer a similar product. Cutting from the fret should be done with a heavy-duty blade or pair of sharp tin snips, while being watchful of not bending the icons, as they'll be near impossible to correct. A good, fool-proof plan is to cut well away from the edge and to then trim the waste material back using a fine needle file. It's often wise to check the fit of components before committing yourself by applying glue and this exercise is no exception. On doing so, I realized that the printed motifs would still show from under the new parts, being about 0.5mm too large. This excess paint must be removed by gently scraping it away with a very sharp, flat scalpel blade, ensuring that the main paint scheme is not damaged.

Etched nickel silver or stainless steel parts are much tougher than brass and can be trickier to remove from the fret. Use tin snips or a sharp heavy-duty blade, leaving a little waste to file away to the final shape.

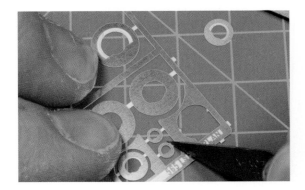

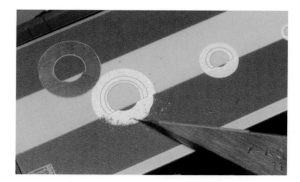

Check that the new part covers the printed graphic completely. If not, use a very sharp blade to gently scrape away any excess, taking care not to damage the paint beneath.

Re-check the icons and then decant some slow-setting superglue on to some scrap card, dabbing a couple of miniscule drops on to the rear of the new part. Be aware that, once in place, any excess glue will be squeezed out of the sides, so just the minimum amount, placed well away from the edges, should be used. Pop it into place, make any adjustments and then leave for a few minutes to set; the slow-setting glue (aim for a 15–20s bonding time) will allow for some final tweaks in position before it 'grabs' the part. On the off-chance that some errant glue finds its way on to the paintwork, try and remove it *tout de suite* with a clean cotton bud, kept at hand just in case. If already set, then wait until it has hardened completely before very carefully scraping it away with a flat blade or fibreglass scratch brush, and a very little T-Cut automotive finish restorer can help revive the paintwork. However, try and avoid this happening in the first place by using the minimum of glue!

The same process is followed for the fitting of etched locomotive nameplates that may or may not have been supplied as separate items within your model's packaging. Sets of etched brass or anti-tarnish stainless steel nameplates are available from numerous sources such as Fox Transfers or Modelmaster Decals. Some makers, such as Shawplan, specialize in D&E-era subjects and, according to the size and intricacy of the prototype, can be relatively inexpensive.

NAMEPLATES

The key to fitting the nameplates properly is to:

(a) remove them from the fret without distortion;
(b) fit them in the right place and completely straight; and
(c) not to overdo the glue and cause excess to ooze out on to the bodywork.

When adding any new components, the minimum of glue is essential to avoid spillage. Decant the glue on to a scrap of card and use a sharp cocktail stick to add a few tiny blobs to the part, as close to centre as possible to limit any 'squeeze-out'.

The larger of the Channel Tunnel logos is built-up from two separate layers. Ensure the base is firmly stuck in place before adding the overlay. Where absolute accuracy is needed, use slower setting superglue to allow time for repositioning and adjustment.

The latter consideration has already been discussed, while problem (a) is resolved by never attempting to use a blade to cut away the fret 'tangs', using the tin snips mentioned above. Problem (b) is quite easy to overcome, if simply covering a printed version of the name, provided that the new plates are not any smaller.

This was the case on a Vi-Trains' Class 37, illustrated here, where the etched *Glendarroch* names proved to be 3mm shorter than the printing that I was trying to conceal. This left me having to scrape away a few millimetres of the originals and I'll describe how to do this in Chapter 5. As for keeping them straight, the best way that I've found to achieve this is to mark out a straight line with a strip of masking tape. The plate can be fixed along the edge of the tape, which is then removed without leaving any marks on the paintwork.

Take no risks when cutting nameplates from their frets. Using a good pair of sharp tin snips is an ideal way of avoiding creasing the metal. File away any excess material to leave nice, smooth edges.

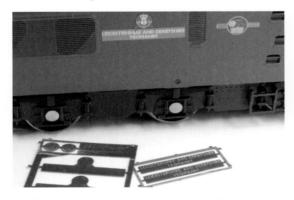

Bachmann often include a set of etched nameplates to compliment some of their christened locomotives. This set is designed to be built-up from two layers to achieve the correct degree of relief.

Although the printed nameplates lack the essential relief of the real thing, when they incorporate an elaborate insignia such as this, it's a shame to cover them with a plainer etched version. Therefore, I opted to just add the main name board to this Class 46.

Even like-for-like replacements may still need a little extra work to fit correctly. This etched nameplate, from Fox Transfers, shows the printed version on the Vi-Trains' model to be a few millimetres too long. A little scraping and touching-in of paint will disguise this.

GOING A LITTLE BIT FURTHER

Danish firm Heljan were first to produce a true-scale model of the Brush re-engineered Class 57 diesel-electric, in 2004, although this is currently out of production. Previously, Lima had simply rebranded their Class 47 without making any detail modifications. However, only Bachmann have had a stab – and a very successful one – at portraying one of the Virgin 'Thunderbirds' fitted with retractable 'Delner' couplings, used for the towing of Pendolino sets during diversions or engineering work.

Having studied the real things, however, there are a couple of control hoses, one either side of the coupler, that do not feature on the model, nor are they supplied with the detailing extras. I can see why these aren't fitted, as they link the chassis to the body, thus making dismantling difficult, but instating them from lengths of brass wire makes a huge visual impact. Reels of soft brass, copper and nickel wire are available from a variety of modelling material suppliers and, while I'm very particular about the straight, stiff wire that I use for handrails and the like, I find that packs of the softer stuff can be picked up much cheaper from stores dealing in jewellery

making. The Hobbycraft chain is a good source for this, although a small craft shop should also stock a range of gauges (diameters).

Form a few short lengths of 0.7mm soft wire into shape with a pair of round-nose pliers and a set of holes drilled in the 57's bufferbeam will fix them in place. Don't secure them to the 'Delner', though. Simply fold them into the space behind it and leave them loose, thus allowing the body to be removed for maintenance; the soft wire will permit being moved about endlessly without breaking. To represent the distinctive pipe unions, cut some thin strips of masking tape (about 1.5mm wide) and wrap around the wire, securing permanently with a drop of superglue. A little paint finishes the job.

And here you've taken your first steps in customizing without even having to remove the locomotive's bodyshell, plus you've scratch-built your own detailing parts. So, after giving yourself a pat on the back, the next step is to begin to use your own judgement to determine whether any other simple enhancements can be made to these, or other, models without any dismantling work. Following that, we can address a glaring omission from the majority of model locomotives: a lack of interior detail and footplate crew.

Using some 0.7mm soft brass wire, the missing pair of hoses from a 'Delner'-fitted Class 57 can be bent to shape using round-nose pliers with some strips of masking tape added to replicate the hose unions, secured permanently with superglue. Don't fix the hoses to the body, as it will make access to the inside difficult.

The new pipes only have to be painted and the unions picked out in yellow and red to finish the job.

Virgin's Class 57 'Thunderbird' rescue locomotives have been modelled by Bachmann and Heljan, although only the former has included the distinctive 'Delner' couplings mounted to the cab. Installing the extra hoses adds something extra to an already striking model.

Locomotive 'Disc' Headcodes

When BR ordered the first batches of diesel locomotives in the late 1950s, a method of train identification was required. Following steam-age practice, the positioning of lights on the front of the engine would describe the classification, and this information was essential to signalmen and other railway staff. With the new forms of traction, it would have been inappropriate to continue using oil lamps, so locomotives were constructed with an array of electric marker lights, situated in a similar pattern to the lamp brackets on a 'steamer'. Circular steel discs, hinged across the centre, were placed over each light and, when opened, the disc would reveal a bright white surface with a hole allowing the light to shine through. When folded closed, the half-disc shape would blend into the body colour and obscure the lamp lens.

The combination of lights shown described the trains' class, these ranging from 0 to 9, and relayed load types, proposed speeds, express or stopping nature and what proportion of the train was equipped with continuous brakes. Dating from the 1880s, lamp codes differed between the independent (and subsequent Big Four) railway companies. BR had standardized the lamp codes in 1950, with only the Southern Region keeping its own unique system. However, the 'standard' codes had been altered slightly by 1972 in order to reflect changing traffic flows on the railways. Despite this, the practice of displaying headcodes fell by the wayside by the late 1970s, as power signalling made it obsolete.

Modellers purchasing a locomotive with this type of headcode are provided with packs of open and

This is a Class 1 train; either an express passenger or newspaper train. The same code could also mean a breakdown train, snow plough, a light engine on its way to assist a disabled train or an officer's special that is not booked to stop within the section.

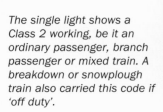

The single light shows a Class 2 working, be it an ordinary passenger, branch passenger or mixed train. A breakdown or snowplough train also carried this code if 'off duty'.

In the original standard BR codes, this display referred to both Classes 3 and 4. Empty stock, parcels or perishable loads, such as fish, fruit, livestock or milk, were classed as Class 3, as long as all vehicles conformed to coaching stock specification. Class 4 meant an express freight train fitted throughout with automatic brakes ('fully-fitted'). Post-1970, only Class 3 carried this code and it referred to parcels trains permitted to travel at 90mph or over.

This display, before 1970, meant a Class 5 express freight train with automatic brakes operative on at least half of the wagons. Later, it described a Class 6 fully-fitted freight, parcels or milk train.

In the 1970 classification of headcode positions, this display referred to an empty coaching stock train, Class 5.

From 1970, this was a Class 7 express non-fully-fitted freight, although it had earlier been used to denote a Class 6 express freight train with automatic brakes operative on not fewer than 20 per cent of wagons.

Originally, this was a Class 7 express unfitted freight train but by 1970 had been re-classified as a Class 8 ordinary freight.

This code ended up having two very different meanings: firstly a Class 8 through unfitted freight; then superseded by the category of Class 4 Freightliner, parcels or express freight permitted to run at 75mph or over.

This position has always referred to the slowest freight service, the humble Class 9 pick-up branch freight. It was also shown on officer's specials or ballast trains due to stop within the section.

Class 0: single or multiple 'light' engines, hauling no more than two brake vans.

A display of all four headcode discs and lights was traditionally used only when hauling the Royal Train. The thickness of the moulded discs is discernible in this view.

closed discs, allowing any desired arrangement to be fitted. Many of these moulded discs are designed to be a friction-fit, negating the use of glues and permitting the codes to be altered at will. A drawback of these mouldings, however, is that they're often a bit too thick and, in some cases, oversized in diameter. The obvious remedy is to add etched replacements but this isn't always a straightforward swap, especially when the originals are too big. Models, such as Bachmann's Class 20 or 40, which incorporate mounting clips above and below the discs, will be set too far apart and this can ruin the effect of adding better-quality components. I'll address this problem in Chapter 7 but, in the mean time, let's have a look at the potential benefits of adding etched brass discs to a Hornby Class 31.

As before, it's essential to prime and paint the new parts while they're still fixed to the fret, a white undercoat being enough for the open discs and the closed ones coloured to suit the cab of the locomotive in question. Being of flat section, there's no mounting lug, and a tiny slither of plastic, fixed underneath the discs, will help to fix them in place on uneven surfaces. Otherwise, it's simply a matter of gluing whichever discs you like to the front of the engine, choosing the pattern to suit the class of train it will be used for. The permanence of superglue means that the facility for changing codes is lost unless a temporary fixing method is devised. Something like Tacky Wax may be used, but this wouldn't stand much handling before the little white discs go flying away into oblivion.

A small detailing job that makes a big impression is the replacement of moulded discs with etched-brass parts. This pack, from Shawplan, provides plenty of open and closed discs that should be primed and painted before fitting.

This Hornby Class 31, already an excellent model, is enhanced by adding new headcode discs. Etched discs have also been fitted to both the Class 40 and Class 44 locomotives featured here.

CHAPTER 4

Interior Design

The interior of a diesel or electric locomotive's cab is often a highly visible space and ready-to-run models that come supplied with a driver are, unfortunately, in the minority. This is a great shame, especially when considering the lengths that manufacturers are going to in their quests to render other details correctly. Indeed, the cab interior mouldings on some of Hornby's machines, such as the Classes 08, 31, 56 and 60, are truly spectacular. Moreover, certain Class 31s even feature distinctive toffee apple-shaped control handles, despite being barely visible from outside. Seats with delicately moulded armrests, control handles, dials and gauges, plus detailed bulkheads with their attendant equipment cabinets and cable conduit, are all in place, but not a driver in sight.

Models that have been around for a little longer have either a very crude representation of the cab or nothing at all. Clearly, there's plenty

of scope for improvement in this area of r-t-r models.

RAILWAY STAFF

There are plenty of cast or moulded figures on the market, encompassing a range of periods, and this brings me on to the subject of uniforms. In the early days of BR diesel and electric traction, the driver would have come from a steam background and would be wearing an outfit of light blue cotton overalls, complete with grease-top cap. Some men even persisted with maintaining the use of an oily rag at the interface between hand and control handle. Soon, though, with BR's drive for a visibly modern railway, drivers received a suitable new costume. From here came the white shirt, blue jacket and tie, plus the distinctive slab-sided blue cap.

Apart from a few minor changes, this costume

Hornby's Class 08 has a fantastic interior that deserves to be shown off. Luckily, the cab doors can be opened and, on this example, I've added an Aidan Campbell standing figure.

Painting figures is one of those chores for which I have to be in the right mood. That's why I usually wait until I've a few to do at once and then knock them out in production line fashion.

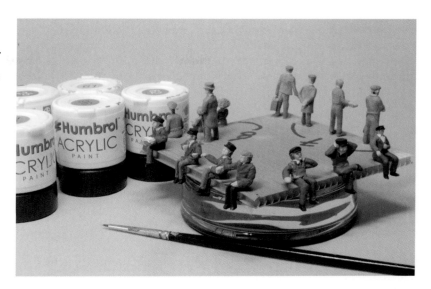

lasted until the end of BR and the move to privatized train operating companies (or TOCs) brought about a veritable rainbow of staff colour schemes, usually in harmony with the new colours of the trains themselves. With modernity also came a more casual approach for some TOCs, particularly freight hauliers: the likes of EWS and Freightliner going for the unimaginative and largely unflattering combo of polyester polo shirt, fleece jacket and baseball cap. In contrast, the majority of passenger-moving operators have introduced some very smart uniforms, predominantly in sober colours, although the driver's hat is no longer a commonly worn garment. The now ubiquitous orange high-visibility vest is also commonly worn by drivers, even while sitting at the controls. Older 'high-vis' wear, by the way, consisted of a much paler orange–yellow bib without the reflective silver strips seen on today's vests.

It should be remembered that, with pre-1970s traction, a 'secondman' was needed to monitor the oil-fired boiler and associated controls. This chap often wore slightly less formal attire than his driver, as an indication of his subordinate nature. Other secondman duties were to be found on freight workings where shunting was involved or when working a branch with manually-operated crossings and ground frames. A goods guard may also be found in the rear cab, keeping an eye on the following wagons during transit. Most of these staffing arrangements evaporated in the 1980s as steam heating, pick-up freights and loose-coupled freight workings all disappeared and single-manning became the norm.

FILLING THE CABS

The ease of accessing the cabs to fit a crew member or two depends on the model in question. Some are devilish to get into, with the potential for damaging delicate lighting units, while others are deceptively simple. Either way, a few precautions should be taken before attempting access. Primarily, if you still have the maintenance instructions with your model, they should illustrate where the necessary screws are to be found that will release the body. Alternatively, some models may have a body that simply unclips. However the model is assembled, be sure to have a good idea of what it is you need to do before jumping in with both feet.

I've chosen to illustrate the method for accessing the interior of one of the more recent Class 56 models, as this is typical of Hornby's new diesel-outline products. Here, the cab mouldings incorporate sprung brass contacts that transfer power to the fibre-optic channels leading to the headlamps and this clever system negates the need to disconnect any electrical connections. It's imperative, however, that these contacts and light assemblies are not damaged during disassembly, being tricky things to repair. Other manufacturers, such as Bachmann, have the cab interior attached to the chassis and independent of the body, although some lighting units may need to be disconnected.

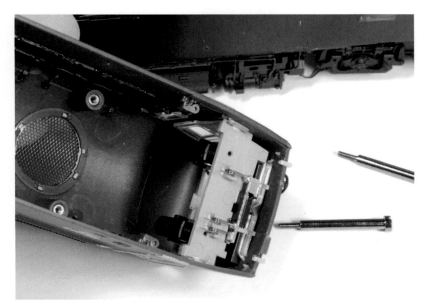

Getting inside Hornby's newer locomotives usually consists of removing four screws, partially obscured by the bogies, and lifting away the bodyshell. A system of fine brass spring contacts beneath the cab interiors is employed, working to relay power to the lights, as seen here on a new Class 56 model. This allows the body to be removed without having to disconnect any wiring.

The Class 56 cab interior can be carefully removed by loosening the glued joint at the sides with a blade, then prising the moulding out. A handy way of keeping the lighting units in place whilst working on the cabs is to stick a few blobs of Tacky Wax, from Deluxe Materials, around them. This is a temporary and non-staining adhesive that will prevent any parts from working loose.

Once the cab interior is revealed, you'll be able to assess how much enhancement work is required. You may want to keep in mind that if you couldn't see part of the interior before revealing it now, it still won't be visible once the body is back on, so think carefully about what it is worthwhile to do. Some painting may be required, particularly picking-out bulkhead details or rendering the false floor black to give a heightened sense of depth.

Fitting expressive and idiosyncratic-looking figures adds real interest and humanity to models and, in my opinion, the range of miniatures produced by Aidan Campbell are among the best available. There's a wide choice of eras, postures and poses, all suitable for drivers, secondmen or guards (amongst many other railway passengers and personnel). Some are even sipping a cuppa or browsing through newspapers. Another source for miniature figures is Dart Castings, from whom a very good-quality selection is available, although these are aimed more towards the steam era.

The Class 56 interiors are already beautifully detailed but some appropriate figures and assorted junk add the final touch. This is a detailing pack from the Ten Commandments range aimed at enhancing model vans and trucks, but equally useful for locomotives. Various magazines are provided, along with newspapers, clipboards and even road maps should your driver take a wrong turn!

Most figures require painting before fitting and they will also probably need trimming in order for them to squeeze into their seats. Use a pair of end-cutters to chop off any limbs that may be too long. The armrest of a chair may also need to be sacrificed to accommodate a wide pair of hips. Once the staff are in place, some other particulars may be added: newspapers and magazines are a good thing to have strewn about the cabs, along with a flask, kit bag, coat or even a 'high-vis' vest draped over an empty seat.

BUILDING AN INTERIOR

Fabricating a cab interior can be a straightforward task, as long as the new parts do not interfere with the mechanism or other internal fittings. Certain Lima and older Hornby models, with their large motorized bogies, leave little space at one end of the bodyshell. With careful measuring and fitting, this is not an insurmountable obstacle.

Dealers in Hornby or Heljan spare parts are able to offer separate cab mouldings at very reasonable prices and, with some cutting, drilling and filing, can be adapted to fit most spaces. I've found the Hornby Class 47 cab mouldings to be very versatile, and these have found their way

Modelling putty, such as Milliput, is perfect for sculpting coats, high-visibility vests and crew baggage. Work on a scrap of card and, once painted, the garments can be peeled off and added to the cabs.

The large front windows of the Class 67 provide an ideal opportunity to detail the cab interior as much of it will be visible. However, many older models may have only a rudimentary cab moulding (if at all). Here, I used a spare Hornby Class 47 moulding, cut to fit within the chassis and painted; the discarded 'high-vis' vest completes the picture.

into all sorts of locomotives, such as the Class 67 illustrated here. On this model, however, the gear towers for each bogie do not allow much space for a depiction of any bulkhead detail. Filling the foreground with a correctly attired driver, a spare 'high-vis' vest and some discarded tabloids, will take attention away from any missing features.

Just as with adding more prototypical exterior details, being familiar with the layout of the real thing is a boon to any modeller. A few images of cab interiors are provided here to spark a little inspiration and, from these, it will be appreciated that some standards exist, such as lighter shades for the upper parts of the interior walls, while the control desks wear a suitable colour to contrast with the controls and dials, making them clearly visible. Colour-coded conduit and fittings are characteristic of the bulkhead areas behind the driver and, if it's possible to do so, reproducing this adds an attractive feature.

LEFT: This view shows the interior of the pioneer Class 37, D6700. This is the 'No.1' end and the driver's controls have been supplemented by modern radio equipment, a sign of its pre-preservation use with English, Welsh and Scottish Railway (EWS).

RIGHT: A contrast in colour scheme is the cab of Class 50, 50033, sporting a rather vivid shade of blue on the control console. Note the large tinted Perspex sun visor above the front window.

LEFT: Bulkheads separating the cab from the engine room often carried important components, such as this Automatic Warning System (AWS) valve and electrical isolation switch, found behind the driver in the cab of Class 40, D200. Colour-coded conduits are an important and distinctive feature to capture.

RIGHT: Some models do have a representation of the various cab fittings but may have been left unpainted. Bachmann's Class 08, for example, has a pleasing amount of detail inside but only once painted does it spring to life.

LEFT: Bachmann's Class 24/25 models greatly benefit from picking-out the moulded interior detail, especially on the cab bulkhead, with appropriate colours.

A distinctive feature of some prototypes is the fitting of large sun visors mounted on scissor-type mechanisms. The Class 92 is one such fleet and this can be reproduced using black cartridge paper, marking out the blinds and drawing the springs with a fine pencil.

Use a clear-setting PVA-based glue to fix the blinds in place. Cut the blinds a bit longer than needed and apply the glue to the waste material. Allow to set completely before refitting the body.

All locomotive cabs possess some form of sun visor and a couple of variations can be discerned in the accompanying photographs of the Class 37 and 50 interiors, being similar in principle to those found in a motor car. More recent traction designs, as well as refurbished machines, now feature roller-type blinds that are clearly visible from the outside. Classes 91 and 92, plus the DRS fleet of rebuilt Class 37s are a couple of examples so fitted and, with a few bits of black paper and a pencil, the blinds can be readily recreated in miniature.

For some locomotive models, scratchbuilding is the best way of achieving a credible interior; a good example of this is the diminutive Bachmann Class 04, coming ready-fitted with a driver figure perched inside an otherwise empty cab. As with all shunting locomotives, there are windows on all four sides, rendering this bareness highly visible. Using a suitable photograph of the interior of a real 04 as a guide, I built up

The colour of the pencil lines should modestly mimic the metal springs, while having the blinds set at different heights adds a bit of individuality.

Another locomotive with generous windows is the Class 04 shunter and Bachmann's model lacks interior detail. A control desk can be quickly fashioned from plastic channel and brass wire.

The painted control desk and bulkhead cabinet have been fitted in place, along with a superior driver.

a rudimentary control desk from Evergreen ⅛in (3.2mm) plastic channel (ref.264), keeping the flat surface sitting uppermost. A few pieces of 0.45mm brass wire were glued into pre-drilled holes to represent the control levers, of which there are numerous on the real thing. Two pieces of the same channel were fixed side by side on the front bulkhead, between the front windscreens, and this formed the bank of gauges and dials. Once glued in place, along with a superior cast white-metal driver, the cab of the model instantly looks much better. Swapping the thick moulded glazing also helped, the side windows being left in an open position to allow the new interior to be seen.

OTHER INTERIOR DECOR

The majority of diesel and electric locomotives, especially those built prior to 1970, boasted

According to prototype, a locomotive type may have various colour-coded conduit visible through the engine room windows and Hurst Models produce this pack of white-metal castings for the Class 47. Each of the four parts is different and painting and fitting instructions are supplied.

windows at various points along the sides of the bodyshell to cast light into the engine and equipment rooms. Usually, an internal corridor linked both cabs and permitted full mechanical access for monitoring and maintenance. These were often very restricted spaces and a system of internal lighting was also provided. Naturally, this means that some of the mechanical and electrical machinery became visible through these windows, along with the attendant series of colour-coded conduits fitted to the engine-room walls and passing directly behind the glass windows.

Both the Hurst and A1 Models' ranges include suitable packs of engine-room window details for specific locomotive types, and simply require

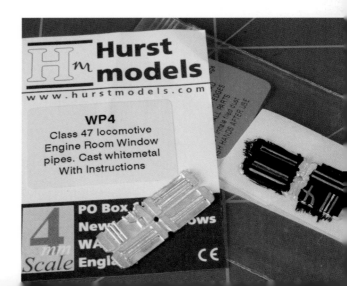

The painted pipework looks ultra-authentic and also disguises the mechanism and wiring inside this Lima model. Unfortunately, the large cast chassis block of the more recent Bachmann 47 means that these castings can't be fitted.

priming and painting before fixing in place. A thoughtful inclusion with the Hurst products is a diagram showing which of the various pipe patterns should fit behind which aperture, and what colour they should be to ensure complete accuracy.

Engine-room windows could actually be opened on some locomotives to permit extra ventilation for anyone moving through or working inside. These must have been welcome for secondmen working on the steam-heat boilers or brewing up on a hotplate provided inside the bowels of the engine, as was the case with original batches of Class 31s. There were even toilets fitted to some traction types and I can't think of anywhere I would least like to answer the call of nature (or make a cup of tea for that matter) than inside an incredibly noisy and smelly machine. That's perhaps why many of these 'facilities' were phased-out on later designs. Regardless, having the odd open window, on an appropriate traction type, is another interesting facet to model, perhaps having something of interest going on inside.

There's certainly no doubt that adding just a few enhancements on the inside goes a long, long way to improving any model, even those that are of an already high standard of fixture and finish.

A1 Models also produce some etched engine room pipework for various locomotive classes and this pack, for the Class 40, has been painted and weathered slightly before fitting. Remember to use odour-free superglue when working near clear glazing.

CHAPTER 5

A Number or a Name

Why take an expensive new model and then mess around with solvents and sharp implements, trying to remove the lovely printed characters or logos that the manufacturer has taken great pains to apply to a very high standard? It can be about a quest for authenticity or broadening a locomotive fleet, perhaps to include a fondly-remembered machine.

To all intents and purposes we, as consumers, are at the mercy of manufacturers in terms of what we can buy off-the-shelf. Despite firms consulting customers as to what type of models should be added to their ranges, it's rare indeed that they would ask whether a seemingly anonymous machine should be produced within this product line. Why, for example, has 37032 never been in the Bachmann or Vi-Trains' catalogues? There's nothing very special about this 37 other than the fact that I used to see it regularly around Warrington in 1985. I even have a photograph of myself, ensconced in a fur-lined anorak, standing cheerily next to the real thing on Bank Quay station; a nostalgia-filled image for me, but meaning little to anyone else.

Some model firms offer only a limited number of models each year within each class so, hypothetically, Bachmann may only offer a total of around four versions of the Class 47 per year, that's a total of twenty examples over a five-year period. Even accounting for extra limited-edition commissions, this will only account for a tiny percentage of a fleet numbering over several hundred. And, on the off chance that your favoured loco is chosen as a subject, would it be offered in green, blue, Railfreight grey or EWS red?

To their credit, other (smaller) concerns, such as Heljan and Vi-Trains, may offer the market a smaller catalogue range but this is countered by their flexibility in terms of number and livery variations. These are produced in small batches so the modeller may have to move quickly to secure a particular item, but this extra choice is certainly welcome. Heljan, in particular, have recently been offering their Class 47 in un-numbered condition, with packs of transfers to be adorned by the customer; virtually every livery ever worn by this locomotive class has been marketed at some point.

All this leaves us with the prospect of having to take a more hands-on approach in order to get hold of whatever particular locomotive that you may desire. There are some model shops, and, indeed, model-makers, who offer a bespoke renumbering service but I can assure you that there is no 'black art' to achieving a professional finish. Years of trial and error have allowed me to fine-tune a method that I'm happy with and willing to endorse, although I am aware that others do exist. I've heard people talk about using brake fluid and other toxic chemicals, but I've never felt the need to try these, not least as some of them sound rather perilous to my own, and the model's, health.

One thing to keep in mind before changing a model's identity is the suitability of the donor model. If authenticity bothers you, check whether the correct detail patterns are carried, such as headcode variant, grille arrangement, period condition and so on. A little research will be helpful, preferably with the result of some decent images from which to refer. Positioning of running numbers, logos and overhead warning signs could differ markedly between individual machines, and getting these small details right can make a big difference.

HOW TO DO IT

Only a small number of materials are required to do the job, the biggest outlay will be in acquiring a good airbrush and compressor with which to apply the sealing coats of varnish at the end. It can't be overstated how important this final step is in blending-in the new decals and disguising any patch-repainting; it's a real make-or-break moment. More information about airbrushes and varnish is provided in Chapter 11.

My own renumbering tool-kit is illustrated here and consists of but a few items. Further to what appears in the photograph are a supply of super-fine wire wool (00000grade) and some tiny strips of 1,000grade wet/dry abrasive paper. These are kept at hand to remove any small scratches that might develop from my own carelessness and, if things are going to plan, are not always required. As far as chemicals go, I have used both white and methylated spirits but these

can have some minor side-effects. The water-like viscosity also means that it's easy to apply too much solvent at once and capillary action is a wonderful, fascinating thing to behold, except when spirits are running uncontrollably into lots of nooks and crannies. By and large, the spirit will evaporate harmlessly without softening any paint or glue joints, although meths does tend to leave behind a whitish stain if the surface is not cleaned quickly.

Despite using these liquids happily for the last few years, I've come to rely, almost solely, on a bottle of T-Cut automotive finish restorer. I had bought this to enliven the paintwork on my increasingly tatty old car but, after talking with other modellers at a show, I was regaled by its usefulness in removing factory-applied characters and logos. My car is still scruffy but my renumbering technique has been sped-up markedly and it seems to work equally well across all manufacturers' products, with only one exception. As will be explained further on in this chapter, the identity of a Vi-Trains' Class 37 is difficult to change and T-Cut only serves to bring the paint off, so watch out!

The practical technique is simple, but does require a degree of care and patience. A large

The tools of the trade, as far as renumbering r-t-r stock is concerned, are a very humble collection. White spirit or methylated spirit can be effective but, through experience, I've found T-Cut automotive paint restorer to be the best softening compound on all but Vi-Trains' models. A ready supply of good quality cotton buds, cocktail sticks, a very sharp blade and a fibreglass brush completes my 'kit'.

supply of cocktail sticks and cotton buds should be kept in stock, as these are the main tools to be used. Good-quality buds are essential, as cheaper ones will leave fibres everywhere and will not keep their shape or absorbent properties for very long. It's helpful to blunt the tips of the cocktail sticks by rubbing them on a hard surface to prevent scratching the model. By dipping the end of the stick into the T-Cut, the viscous fluid will stick to the wooden tip and this can then be transferred to the work area.

By gently rubbing the printed numerals with the side of the stick's tip (not the end of the tip – *see* photograph below) the T-Cut will soon start to cause the printing to diminish. As the solution becomes contaminated with softened paint, mop it up with a bud and clean the stick with tissue or a rag. A clean blob of T-Cut can then be added and the process repeated until the offending characters have gone. Another benefit of this fluid is that it is quite thick and tends not to drip away to other, unwanted areas; this permits the odd digit or small icon to be removed without affecting surrounding areas. As an insurance measure, however, masking tape may be used to protect any characters that are to be retained.

A word of warning must be added here, in regard to attempting to change only part of a factory-applied number set. In the factory, a 'tampo' printing machine is loaded with paint and this is pressed on to the model, leaving behind the logotype or number and so on. The nature of this method of production means that the 'weighting' of digits or numerals can sometimes be a little heavier than scale measurements would dictate and also creates inconsistencies between batches. Now, these variables can all be measured in fractions of a millimetre and, as a result, you may think they need not be considered. However, when applying new decals that have been produced by a wholly different process, using inks instead of paint, there is going to be a visible discrepancy. Included overleaf is an image of a Hornby Class 60 that has had the last two digits of its TOPS (Total Operations Processing System as used by BR) number altered using Fox waterslide transfers, and it can be discerned that the new digits are ever-so-slightly shorter and lighter in 'weight' than the printed originals. Therefore, I'd always advocate changing the whole number in all cases, as the extra work involved is negligible compared to the quality of the finished result.

Before applying a new set of decals, the surface should be cleaned of any remaining T-Cut and then buffed-up with a clean bud and a toothbrush, the nylon bristles of which produce a burnishing action and thus remove any minor scratches that may have been caused. The result is a pleasant glossy finish that is perfect for a new set of transfers to sit on.

Decant a little T-Cut into a receptacle, dip in a cocktail stick and then proceed to rub the offending digits lightly with the side of the stick (not the pointy tip). Depending on the model, this should take only a few minutes before the printed characters begin to disappear. Don't try and rush this – there are no shortcuts! Mop up the contaminated liquid regularly with a cotton bud and add more clean T-Cut, wiping the stick on a tissue to keep it clean. Eventually, all of the printed characters will have been removed and the surface can be cleaned with buds and then buffed with an old (but clean) toothbrush.

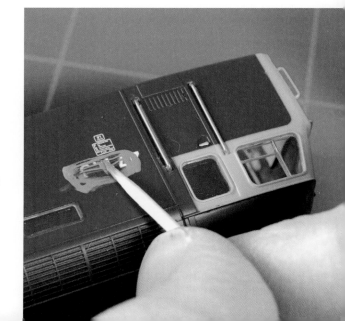

It's always preferable to remove the entire running number from a locomotive and start from scratch, as trying to match transfers to factory-printed characters is difficult. Look closely at the last two digits on the sides and front of this Hornby Class 60 and you'll see that they're slightly smaller and thinner.

TRANSFER TYPES

There are three main types of model decal: waterslide, 'rub-on', and pressfix/methfix. The waterslide variety are probably most familiar to most modellers, especially those who grew up building Airfix kits, and the ranges of Fox Transfers and Modelmaster Decals are the leading sources of BR and Privatization subjects.

The benefit of T-Cut then becomes apparent as the model's surface will have developed a glossy sheen after buffing, perfect for the new decals to adhere to.

Other sources include Hurst Models' 'Trainsfer' range, Replica Railways and Precision Labels. Complete, ready-assembled number sets are available, along with packs of individual digits. Fox also offer almost-complete sets that only require the final one or two characters to be added; these packs make application and alignment quicker and simpler.

Waterslide decals are simple to apply, being printed on to a clear carrier film that floats away from the backing paper after soaking for a short while in clean water. The decal is then trans-

The same 'T-Cut method' can also be used to correct small printing errors, such as correcting the overhead warning flashes, especially to 1960s-condition locomotives, which tend to appear with post-1980s style stickers. If the surface is sufficiently 'shiny' after buffing, apply replacement waterslide decals, manipulating with a blunt cocktail stick and soaking-up excess water with cotton buds.

ferred from the paper to the model, positioned and then dried using cotton buds. An important point to remember is that a high-gloss finish is an essential basis on which to place these decals, if the carrier film is not to be visible. The T-Cut method described above can result in a pleasant sheen but this may not always be glossy enough for some transfers, especially when working with large icons or on uneven surfaces. One or two coats of a high-quality gloss varnish, applied from an airbrush, is the preferred way to a professional finish, as the shinier the surface, the better the decals will adhere.

The 'rub-on' decals of the Replica Railways range have taken on something of a Holy Grail identity for your author, as this firm's small, white TOPS numbers are my own personal favourite. Unfortunately, they've been out of production for a while, although I believe that they're in the process of being redrawn in digital format for production by a new supplier. As my own stocks of these packs have dwindled, I shall await their release with baited breath, although other packs have already been updated and are available from the Replica stand at model-railway shows around the country. The big advantage of 'rub-on' (or 'rub-down' as some people call them) transfers is the lack of any necessary surface preparation other than the removal of the old characters.

Again, complete number sets are offered, as well as individual digits, and alignment is possible due to the clear backing film. Rubbing is done with a pencil and the new character is sealed in place by rubbing over again with a pencil and tracing paper. The drawback of this method is that, unlike with waterslide decals, no adjustment whatsoever is possible once the transfer has

been applied; it has to be perfect first time. Any errors have to be remedied by scraping away the character and starting again, but this carries a risk of damaging the surface.

Pressfix decals incorporate the better features of both the above types, combining the lack of carrier film of the 'rub-on' with the adjustable qualities of the waterslide. The HMRS (Historical Model Railway Society) range are hard to fault, packs being available for the early and late BR eras (as well as pre-BR, although these are 'general' packs with individual digits only). However, the packs for locomotives also include overhead warning signs, BR double-arrow symbols and other embellishments, making them a one-stop pack rather than having to buy several packs from other manufacturers to finish a single model.

The chosen decal is cut from the dual-layer backing sheet and placed in position, the sticky nature of the paper holding it in place. The paper is translucent to permit alignment and, when satisfied with its location, finger pressure secures it while water is applied with a paint brush. A few seconds later and the backing paper can be floated away and the area dried, any remaining gum being washed away. As with 'rub-ons', no surface preparation is required, save for ensuring that the model is free from grease and dust; even an ultra-matt finish not being at all problematic. The methfix variety of decals work in exactly the same way, but methylated spirit is used to dissolve the backing paper instead of water and this variety boasts a finer level of finish, although working time is sacrificed as each decal requires about ten minutes for the meths to work.

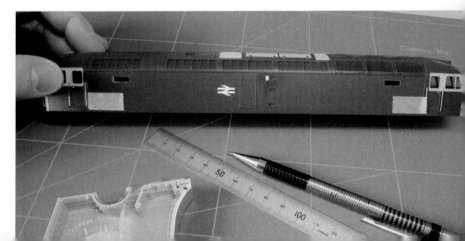

In order to keep the new numerals in a straight line, mark out their locations and apply some small strips of low-tack masking tape to act as guides. Check they're horizontal by measuring against the lower edge of the body.

My preference for transfers is the Pressfix variety produced by HMRS; these are placed on the surface and adjusted until perfectly aligned. A little pressure will hold it in place while a wet brush is applied. The backing paper will then soften and, after a few seconds, can be lifted away.

COLOUR PATCHES

An alternative to physically removing printed locomotive numbers is to cover them using the range of 'obliteration patches' offered by both Fox and Modelmaster. These are available in many different livery colours and Fox, in particular, tailor their packs to suit specific manufacturers' shades. Packs consist of a single patch that requires cutting to size and I've found these useful for repairing small areas of missing paint (where I've been a bit over-eager with the solvents). However, using them solely as intended can have a few disadvantages, as the tampo factory printing process means that the paint is raised up from the surface and no waterslide blanking patch can hide this; no matter how good the colour match is, when the light catches the side of the loco, the old numbers will be seen. As with all waterslide decals, the surface must be given a gloss preparation beforehand, and so this method proves not to be such a shortcut after all.

SPECIAL CIRCUMSTANCES

Replacing printed characters on uneven surfaces can cause several annoying complications, regardless of the methods employed. Whether using white spirit, meths or T-Cut, the undulating nature of the surface means that more pressure, and, invariably, more solvent, comes to bear on the edges of the raised areas, while the inner corners of the recesses are difficult to reach.

A good case study of this is the Class 67 in EWS red/gold livery, as now produced by Hornby. With no detriment intended towards Hornby (the quality of finish to this model is excellent), part of the problem in renumbering is caused by how the livery has been applied in the factory. Most modellers, working from scratch, would apply this EWS scheme by first spraying the whole model in the light 'gold' colour, before masking this off and applying the darker 'red' shade. However, in mass-production methods this is often reversed and the entire shell will be given a coat of red while the lighter colours are applied on top; the EWS markings and numbers then being tampo printed on to the gold. This, combined with the problems of working on uneven surfaces, makes it all too easy to damage the gold paint and to reveal the darker shade beneath.

If this occurs, either an obliteration patch or patch painting is in order. As has been hinted already, matching a correct shade of paint can be difficult as paint makers interpret shades differently and, on schemes such as the EWS livery, it may be more beneficial to re-cover the whole gold area rather than try to repair a small patch.

Seating transfers on to an irregular plane is made easer by:

(a) using the best quality decals; and
(b) inviting the assistance of a decal-softening solution, such as Carr's Transfix or Microsol.

The transfer is placed as usual and pressed down gently into the undulating surface with a cotton bud, ensuring that it remains straight. Once all

Alpha-Numerical Headcodes

Four Characters

The limitations of the traditional lamp or 'disc' methods of train reporting were soon realized and locomotive types already under development or construction in the early 1960s were altered to carry either twin or single display windows on the cab fronts. These were equipped with roller blinds carrying large white numbers or letters on a black background. Light bulbs sat just behind each of the windows to illuminate the four characters. As a result, locomotive types that were built over a prolonged period could feature a range of headcode fitments throughout their fleets. The Class 40, for example, went from batches of disc-fitted fronts to 'split' headcode boxes and then, finally, to single centrally mounted box variants.

The four-character system retained the traditional class codes, denoted by the first digit, although changing traffic patterns and operating procedures meant that some of the meanings of the classes altered. The second character, a letter, would describe the train's destination, while the third and forth characters (numerals) related to the individual service and could be cross-referenced in the working timetables. By their nature, four-character headcodes allowed for countless variations and it would be impossible to list them all here. The destination letters gave up to twenty options, some of which denoted the regions of the BR system where the train was heading towards, whereas others were only used on services that would not stray into other regions and, thus, allowed for duplication.

LEFT: *Finding out a selection of correct headcodes for your layout's period and location can be simple. Looking at period photographs is one way or old 'ABC's such as these can be a goldmine of information. I picked these up from a car boot sale recently, for just 20p!*

BELOW: *Other models, such as this Bachmann Class 37, come with factory-printed headcodes. These can be changed, however, by removing the black plastic insert with a sharp blade. They're usually held in place with only a small amount of glue at each side.*

Here's a selection of the more common of these destination codes:

A   London-bound or London district workings.
E   Eastern Region.
L   East Anglian area.
M   London Midland Region.
N   North-Eastern Region.
O   Southern Region.
S   Scottish Region.
V   Western Region.
X   Royal train or out-of-gauge load.
Z   Special trains.

Other letters such as T, J, H, K or P could be used for local or 'trip' workings that would remain within the same region throughout the journey.

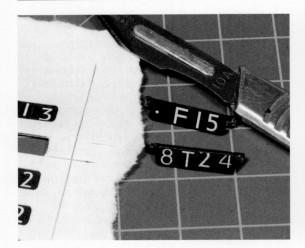

The dimensions of headcode panels varied throughout locomotive types, but the printed codes offered with Heljan's Class 27s are a perfect fit for the Bachmann 37. Stick in place with double-sided tape and touch in the white paper edges.

The newly modified panels can then be pushed back into place and the model reassembled. Retain the panels with a tiny blob of solvent-free glue (such as Tacky Glue from Deluxe) and this will allow further changes without difficulty.

For models with backlit headcode panels, changing the display is not so straightforward. Bachmann's Class 47 can be altered by rubbing the inside of the printed panel with a few drops of T-Cut and a blunt cocktail stick. This may take a good few minutes for each end but it's the only way of working that will not irrevocably damage the clear plastic. Mop up the softened paint with cotton buds regularly and, when clear, buff with a soft cloth.

Replacement backlit headcodes are available from the Precision Labels' range and packs are tailored to specific prototypes. For the Bachmann 47, I used pack ref.BL41D.

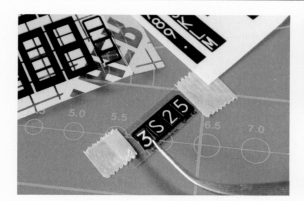

The self-adhesive clear plastic film incorporates printed outlines of the blinds and the individual characters can be cut out and stuck in place, facing upwards.

The self-adhesive film needs some extra 'stickiness' to stay put, so use a couple of blobs of a thick PVA-type glue, keeping it away from the visible area. Allow to set completely before reassembly.

Mounting a few characters in an uneven manner is entirely prototypical as it was rare that a driver would bother to align everything perfectly. With repeated use, blinds were known to become a bit 'wonky' or even stuck, sometimes necessitating a sticker over the front of the panel with the correct character.

Two Characters

Traction types could also carry a two-character headcode; this was the case largely on diesel and electric multiple units, so being outside the remit of this volume. However, some mainline locomotives did employ a twin-character system, such as the Southern Region Class 33 and 73. It's probably possible to fill an entire book on the subject of the Southern's train-reporting codes and, as a Northerner with little interest in this field, I've never really bothered to expend much effort in deciphering it all.

However, I believe that a basic rule-of-thumb is thus: a plain numerical code (i.e. two numbers) was used on electric multiple units or locomotives while working passenger services over 'multiple unit routes'. Diesel locomotives or units working the same services/routes also carried a twin numeral code but with the addition of a short bar above the digits. Alternatively, passenger electric traction running over 'non-multiple unit routes', or moving between regions, carried a letter and a number, while diesels in the same situation, again, did likewise but with the short bar included. To complicate matters, inter-regional workings from or to the Central Division area carried a twin-letter sign.

Empty electric-powered passenger stock or van trains carried their regular code but with a long bar over the numbers; such stock in the charge of diesel traction carried two short bars. Freight services, meanwhile, used a route numeral and letter code for trains that remained within the Southern's boundaries and these did not indicate the class of the service. Inter-regional freights had a twin-letter code, diesel locomotives including a short bar above the characters. Incidentally, the EK code that I've shown being fitted to a Heljan Class 33/1 relates to a freight trip from Temple Mills to Holborough, running via Dartford and the short white bar is correctly shown for this diesel locomotive. (See below.)

This pack of pre-printed headcodes, for a Heljan Class 33, features the two-character Southern Region display. After cutting out the desired code, run a black marker or felt-tipped pen around the edges to hide the white of the paper.

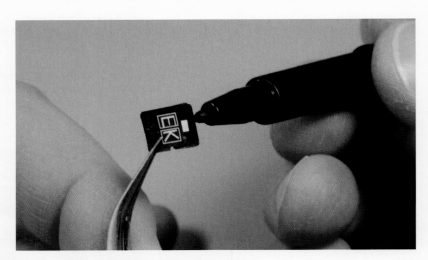

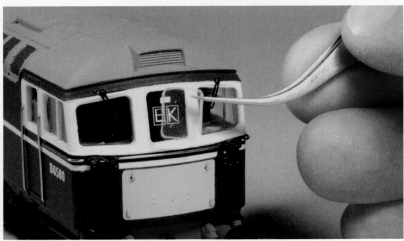

Heljan's models employ a push-fit system to lock the glazing in place over the headcodes. The edges of the clear plastic are chamfered inwards slightly on one face to give a tight fit, so check that the piece is being fitted the correct way around.

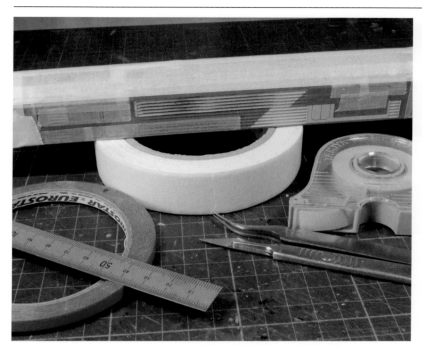

There are times when we all make mistakes, and I was a little too eager with this Class 67, resulting in the base colour showing through. The only way from here is to either apply waterslide livery 'patches' or to effect a patch repaint. For a high-standard finish I went for the latter and masked-up the body to leave all the EWS 'gold' exposed. A good-quality vinyl tape from Electrostar was used to mask-up the immediate area and, being a flexible film, can be manipulated within the rippled bodysides. For economy's sake, less expensive tapes were applied to the rest of the model and all tape joints sealed with Humbrol Maskol fluid.

the water has been soaked up, apply some of the softening solution and wait for a few minutes before very carefully dabbing the decal over the raised detail. The chemicals will serve to temper the brittleness of the decal, allowing it to stretch into any recesses without tearing. Again, check for correct alignment and then allow it to dry naturally overnight.

A light undercoat of Humbrol matt white was sprayed from an airbrush, an aerosol primer being avoided as these tend to go on a bit thick. After applying two thin coats of Railmatch EWS 'gold', the tape was removed and any excess paint escaping through the masking was cleared-up with a white spirit-soaked cotton bud, where necessary.

The whole bodyshell should be given a coat of gloss varnish (masking the glazing if necessary) before the new transfers are applied. An uneven surface can make this a challenging pursuit but these transfers from the Modelmaster range are certainly up to the job. Position them in place with a blunt cocktail stick and dab away the wetness with a cotton bud.

Gently push the transfer into the grooved surface, ensuring that it remains straight. Once the water has been soaked up, brush over a softening fluid such as Transfix. If left for a few minutes, the solvent will help the decal stretch slightly to cope with the surface without ripping. Soak up any excess with a bud and leave to dry naturally before a sealing coat of varnish is applied.

THE VI-TRAINS' AFFAIR

While working on the Mainline blue liveried Vi-Trains' Class 37, featured in Chapter 14, I tried to change the locomotive's number using my trusty 'T-Cut method'. However, even with very light pressure being exerted and the minimum of solvent used, the blue paint quickly evaporated to leave grey primer showing through. Using a tiny amount of white spirit and a cocktail stick was more effective, although not entirely as the paint seems to have been applied so thinly that any interference runs the risk of exposing the undercoat. A tiny spot of weathering will hide the odd imperfection but, with my first effort, I was left with a sizable patch of missing paint.

Patch-repainting was not so hard, as I had to touch-in some new components anyway. The problem was where to limit the new paint without creating an obvious 'seam'. Luckily, the Class 37 has plenty of natural bodywork features with which to create a 'paint break': the door frame, grille and bodyside stripe being utilized. However, we've already talked about the lack of consistency in interpretations of liveries between r-t-r and paint manufacturers, and no matter how well the seam is disguised, the colour will still stand out. Other than re-spraying the whole model, I could only give the machine an overall coat of weathering to hide the discrepancy.

The T-Cut renumbering method works for all brands of r-t-r models, save for the Vi-Trains' Class 37. This is due to the relatively thin coat of paint applied to these models and, having tested the T-Cut, the grey primer was quick to show through. Undaunted, I simply masked-up the affected area and sprayed a light coat of the Mainline Blue (Railmatch Paints) in a similar way to the Class 67.

The Railmatch shade of blue differs from Vi-Trains' interpretation but, once weathering (*see* Chapter 12) had been applied, the inconsistency was disguised.

CHANGING NAMES

A change of locomotive number may also mean a change of name and it's rare that the name-plates of two locomotives will be of the same size. Naturally, when replacing a long name for a short one, some of the printed nameplate will have to be removed. The T-Cut method will do the trick again, although it will take longer to soften this thicker paint. A way of speeding things up is to use a flat, sharp blade to scrape away some of the printed nameplate. Don't try to remove the whole thing in this way as the main paintwork will be damaged, instead finish off with the T-Cut. Take great care here, this being a job for the more experienced modeller.

Accurate fitting of replacement nameplates is critical, if attention is not to be drawn to the

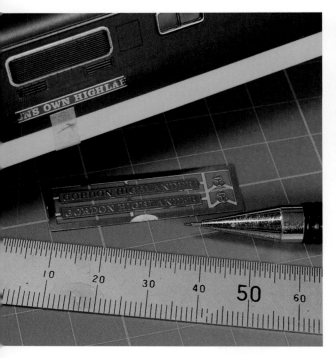

The accurate fitting of nameplates is crucial: measure the centre line of the plate's location as well as the horizontal plane and apply masking-tape guides.

It's doubly important to align things properly if the nameplates are accompanied by something like this regimental crest that must sit exactly central.

model for the wrong reasons. Measure the centre line of the plate's location, as well as the horizontal plane, and apply masking-tape guides. Before doing any of this, however, it may be worth checking that your chosen prototype carried its nameplate in the same place as the original model; variations did exist.

FINISHING OFF THE JOB

Whether new transfers have been added, new nameplates fitted or some new paintwork touched-in, an overall coat of varnish is essential. Glazing units need not be removed as careful masking is acceptable, although the inside of the bodyshell should also be masked to protect from overspray. Depending on your own preferences, a satin or matt coating will serve to blend in any alterations and give the model a truly pro-

fessional finish. On the other hand, a realistic shortcut is to spray a very thin 'misted' layer of matt varnish over only the area where alterations have been made and, if using a good airbrush, the varnish may blend in with the surrounding paintwork. This will rarely give a perfect finish but, if the model is to be weathered in any way, then this should be more than adequate.

If the desired logos or numeral styles are not available as off-the-shelf transfers, making your own decals is now a viable alternative, providing you have access to a computer and a suitable colour printer. Sources, such as Crafty Computer Paper, can supply A4-sized sheets of waterslide or rub-down papers, and a choice of clear or white backing is provided to suit different applications. *See* the Appendix for contact information and website details (from which detailed instructions can be downloaded). I admit to suffering computers as a necessary evil of modern life, so spending time manipulating images and text to the right scale is not really my thing.

Careful dismantling, patient and gentle work with the solvents, accurate alignment of decals and judicious use of varnish will see you through whatever task may be planned. Don't forget that mistakes happen, but nine times out of ten, they can be remedied. And weathering can cover a multitude of sins!

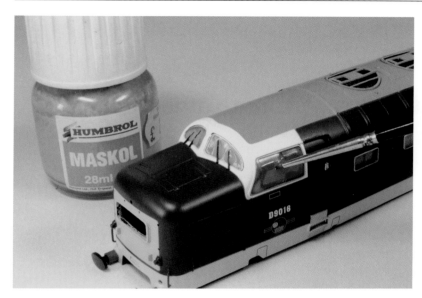

This Bachmann 'Deltic' has been renumbered and named using the T-Cut method, but the glossy sheen and new decals must be blended back into the overall finish. Clean the body of dust or grease and then mask-up the glazing with small strips of tape, sealing with Maskol.

Apply an overall coat of satin or matt varnish, preferably from a good airbrush, and set the model aside overnight to dry before reassembly.

After adding new waterslide overhead warning decals to this Heljan Class 27, a fine misting of matt varnish was sprayed over the new transfers only (having masked the windows) in an effort to blend them in with the surrounding paint finish. As I planned to apply a weathered finish, any discrepancies were hidden.

CHAPTER 6

First Steps in Customizing

Hopefully, you may already be developing more of a critical eye in terms of identifying possible improvements to r-t-r models. We've already looked at making very minor improvements, concentrating largely on adding supplied components, as well as the odd little extra. Here, though, are a few suggested projects to take your skills to the next level.

BUFFERS

One of the first things to grab my attention is the quality, or otherwise, of a model locomotive's buffers. Perhaps it's because they protrude outwards from the 'face' of the model, but they can have quite an impact on the engine's overall appearance. This statement is proved by studying the Vi-Trains' Class 37, which is, by and large, a good model, although it is let down by the feeble-looking plastic things pointing out from the bufferbeam. Swapping these for a set of turned brass components is, literally, a 10min job and the outcome greatly outweighs the short time spent. Extra embellishments, such as footstep treads atop the buffer shanks, also help.

Both sprung and solid replacement buffers are available in brass and nickel steel, in addition to cast white-metal units, from detailing suppliers such as A1, Shawplan, Alexander Models and Craftsman, and differ in cost according to specification (sprung being more costly). As I utilize working scale couplings on my stock, I try to fit sprung buffers wherever possible, as this improves performance. However, most sprung oval buffers carry the same flaw, where the shafts

ABOVE: A good set of buffers can sometimes be the difference between a good model and a great model. The Vi-Trains' Class 37 is a good model in its original form but is marred by the buffers.

BELOW: Conveniently, the Vi-Trains' bufferbeams can be dismantled by removing a pair of screws. Pull out the oval buffer heads and use a pair of end-cutters to chop off the plastic buffer shanks a few millimetres away from the base. Then cut them flush and open-out the mounting holes to suit the diameter of your chosen replacements.

In this case I've fitted a set of turned brass, non-sprung buffers from A1 Models, glued into place with thick, slow-setting superglue. Adding some etched brass chequer plate footsteps to the tops of the shanks makes a nice touch and this is available from Mainly Trains (ref.MT355). Cut some 2 × 2mm squares using tin snips and superglue in place.

are left to rotate freely inside each shank. This allows for a free springing action but also lets the heads turn around too easily, something that the real things certainly don't do. This is far from a problem for round buffer heads, but is a big one for those of an oval or rectangular pattern. There is no simple cure for this and I'd suggest thinking twice before buying a set of deluxe sprung units.

Another consideration regarding sprung buffers is whether there is sufficient space for access behind the bufferbeam to complete the assembly procedure; this is not always possible and depends on the model in question. Regardless of any drawbacks, a good set of sprung heads can't be beaten for looks and operation, especially whilst engaged in careful shunting operations. Brass buffers, in general, have a much lower profile to the heads than cast components and white-metal heads, being rather brittle, can be easily damaged.

Fitting of any new buffers is usually straightforward, the old ones being chopped away with a good pair of end-cutters, such as those made by Xuron for use with model railway track.

By letting these tools cut through the majority of the waste, a sharp blade can then take the material back to sit flush with the bufferbeam. Turned shanks rarely include a representation of the square mounts; separate etched backing plates are available in both the Shawplan and A1 ranges, and some of these can be seen in place on the detailed Class 20 in the following chapter. (*See* page 88.) A suitable hole needs to be provided for the new shanks and any existing hole in the bufferbeam may need opening-out to the necessary diameter. Often, it's best to do this in increments, to prevent a drill from wandering off-centre and leaving a sloppy fit. Measure the mounting lug and then work in 0.5mm steps until reaching the final size.

For sprung buffers, depending on the assembly method, a small nut is often provided to be attached to the threaded shaft after fitting into the shanks. It may be awkward to reach behind the bufferbeam, so use a pair of fine-point tweezers to hold the nut in place, whilst turning the buffer head with the other hand. Keep threading the nut until a sufficient amount of spring travel

When detailing a Bachmann Class 66, the valances slot into place under the chassis and can be retained with some epoxy glue, any gap being packed with model filler. The plastic buffers were cut away and replaced by a sprung set from A1 Models. The brass shanks should be fitted first and, once the glue has set, the steel heads threaded with their springs and inserted. Small nuts are provided to secure the heads from behind the bufferbeam.

This Class 37/5 sports a typical set of three-piece snowploughs. The mounting brackets are visible, while the angle at which the blades are set can also be discerned.

is reached. A tiny blob of Loctite thread sealant will prevent the nut working loose over time without forming an immovable joint.

SNOWPLOUGHS

Two- or three-piece miniature snowploughs were fitted across many BR traction-types during the winter months, if there was a perceived risk of snow along certain routes. Not all locomotives were fitted with suitable brackets, however, and this is another small nugget of prototype data that can be useful to resolve before embarking on fitting a set. Rather like the details of brake fitment to Class 08s mentioned in Chapter 3, such information can be gleaned from specification lists.

Originally, the plough blades wore black in the early 1960s but, with the development of warning panels on cab fronts, received yellow paint. Southern Region locomotives received a specific pattern of ploughs designed to not interfere with live rails, and appropriate mouldings produced by Heljan are included with its Class 33 models, in addition to etched components in the A1 and Shawplan ranges. The latter two firms also produce some splendid products to cater for the regular two- or three-piece sets, and one of these is featured in Chapter 7.

Here, though, is illustrated a moulded plastic set by Heljan, as included with some Class 47

models, and these are also available as spare parts from Howes Models. The set can be left as a single unit or cut away the linking plastic lugs to fit each component separately. Although not boasting the fine profile of etched parts, these mouldings are nonetheless impressive and, once the off-sides have been painted black and the units fitted properly, they do look very effective.

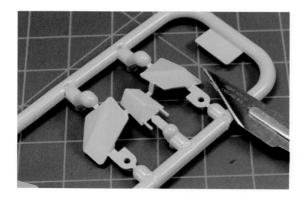

This is the Heljan snowplough sprue as supplied with the Danish firm's Class 47 models and also available as a spare part from Howes Models. The unit can be fitted as a single piece (disguise the links with black paint) or separated and fitted individually for a more realistic look. The side parts are anchored behind the bufferbeams, while the central blade should be glued to the front, the lugs sitting either side of the coupling hook.

Vi-Trains' moulded snowploughs (seen left) are provided in three pieces: the outer two clipping to the bogie frames, while the centre portion fixes to the coupling mount. These can look a bit peculiar when the engine takes a corner, as the central piece stays still while the others swing to the side. The 37 on the right has been modified with a set of Heljan 'ploughs and these remain fixed to the bufferbeam, just like the real thing.

HANDRAILS

Separate handrails and globe-shaped mounting brackets are usually more likely to be found adorning the boiler of a steam locomotive; however, some of the first diesel locomotives shared these fittings. A good example is the humble Drewry-built BR Class 04 0-6-0 diesel-mechanical shunter that originated way back in 1952. A model of this prototype has been produced by Bachmann since 1997, although

its antecedence can be traced back to Mainline's Class 03 model from the early 1980s. The Bachmann product comes supplied with a set of plastic cabside handrails in self-coloured plastic for DIY fitment but are, along with the moulded handrails along the bonnet tops, way over-scale. Some lengths of straight brass wire and a bag of short steam loco handrail 'knobs' can be obtained and fitted instead with pleasing results.

Bachmann's Class 04 comes with moulded plastic handrails and this feature is ripe for development by substituting brass wire and turned mounting knobs. Firstly, the mouldings require cutting away with a sharp blade, working gradually until the old mounts have been cut flush with the surface.

After pushing a punch into the centre of the old handrail brackets locations, a hole can be drilled to suit the shank size of the new components. For this pack of Kemco turned brass brackets, a 1.5mm drill bit was used, working at a consistent angle for each hole.

After the brackets have been glued into their locations (ensuring that the holes are in alignment), 0.4mm handrail wire may be trimmed to length and threaded into place. Using a stiff wire for these situations is important, despite it being a little more expensive than the soft types used earlier.

In previous chapters we've used flexible jewellery wire to form pipes and such but, in the case of handrails, using a higher grade of stiff brass is essential. Alan Gibson offer packs of 250mm lengths of brass in a range of gauges, from 0.33 to 0.9mm and this is among the best available. As for handrail 'knobs', there are plenty of different types to choose from, and quality and sizes can vary. For this project I've employed a pack of Kemco short 'knobs' that have been lying around in my tool-box for ages. These aren't the finest available, but are good nonetheless.

The cutting of handrail wire is best done with a pair of tin snips, rather than end-cutters, as it results in a much cleaner edge, which is important when threading the wire through a small bracket without much clearance; end-cutters tend to flatten the wire near the cut, and having

The power reaches the wheels of the Class 03/04 locomotives via an external final drive, located behind the cab stairs. This obviously presents a hazard for staff riding on the footsteps during shunting and, therefore, a sheet of steel mesh is fixed to the rear of the steps, as seen on this Class 03.

Various types of miniature mesh are available either in the form of etched components or, as featured here, as real miniature mesh! This stainless steel material is offered in the Scale Caliber range from Cammett Ltd and it comes in a range of thread sizes, 60 threads-per-inch being used on my model.

The finished and weathered model has had the new handrails primed and painted to match the bodywork and the bufferbeam valances filled-in following removal of the tension lock couplings. Working three-link couplings have been fitted (see Chapter 8 for more on couplings) and the steel mesh is visible behind the cab footsteps.

to file this extra width away is tiresome. Once the 'knobs' are in place, the wire cut to size and threaded through the mounting holes, a drop of superglue is applied with the tip of a cocktail stick to hold it all in place. By carefully applying an undercoat of matt white or light grey to the new parts, using Humbrol enamels or acrylics, a couple of thin coats of the correct livery can then be brushed on, perhaps followed by a little

matt varnish to unify the new paint with the rest of the finish.

Of course, handrail wire is not only suitable for handrails, but also for other purposes, such as fabricating a set of rear view mirrors, as fitted to some of EWS' Class 66s. When using the wire in this way, i.e. forming a staple shape, a bending jig, such as that designed by Bill Bedford, is indispensible. Small, inexpensive

Class 66, 66147, is seen passing through Dent station in November 2007 and, like many other such machines, it has received a set of low-profile rear-view side-mirrors on the outside of the cabs. These are not featured on any of the Bachmann models, which makes for a simple project.

and simple to use, this jig speeds production of consistently accurate parts. Catering for 100 different sizes between 0.5 and 16.5mm, this should cover all but the longer handrail lengths to be found on diesel and electric locomotives.

Mark out the location of the mirror brackets, checking against prototype photographs, before drilling a set of 0.4mm mounting holes. Take great care not to damage the glazing or loosen it while drilling through, exerting only gentle pressure and letting the drill do the work.

This handrail bending jig, produced by Bill Bedford Models, is ideal for ensuring that components are produced consistently and accurately. Choose the correct gradation according to the length required and fold the 0.3mm wire around the edges, using a set of fine pliers.

A tiny drop of odourless superglue (to protect the glazing) will hold the wire in place. Make sure that the brackets stand proud of the body by about 0.75mm and then cut some strip brass to form the mirror lenses. Mainly Trains supply strips of 0.010in thick brass in 0.040in (1mm) widths and this is perfect, cut to 3mm lengths.

An undercoat of red Humbrol acrylic forms an ideal base for the Railmatch EWS red.

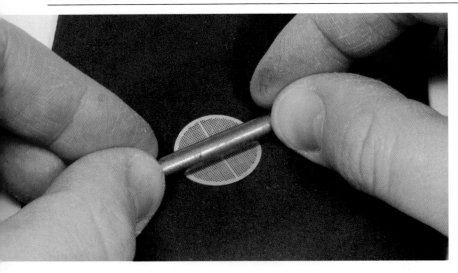

To form a curved profile on an etched-brass component, place the part face down on to the back of a PC mouse mat (or several pieces of kitchen tissue) and roll a steel bar over it, rather like using a rolling pin on pastry. Use gentle pressure and work right to the edges.

CASE STUDY: BACHMANN CLASS 37

Another fundamental of locomotive detailing is the fitting of etched brass grilles in place of inferior or moulded parts. This isn't an operation limited to older models, as a good number of contemporary, high-spec products still offer room for improvement in these areas. We'll look at cutting out big lumps of the bodywork in the next chapter but, before going that far, substituting a roof-mounted radiator fan grille can sometimes be done in a generally non-invasive manner, depending on the model in question.

Bachmann's splendid rendition of an early

Class 37 renders the radiator grille by means of layering mesh between a plastic surround and a fan assembly. While this gives a decent impression of the real set-up, the mesh is coarse and not to scale. Although Shawplan offer a superior twin-piece replacement, produced in 0.010in (0.25mm) brass, to get the new parts to fit, the flat brass components must be shaped to match the curved profile of the roof. By laying the part face down on the rear of a foam computer mouse mat (or several layers of tissue or cloth) and gently rolling over with a metal rod, the brass sheet will begin to take on a curved profile. The degree of curvature is dependant on the amount of pressure exerted; the diameter of the rod is not too impor-

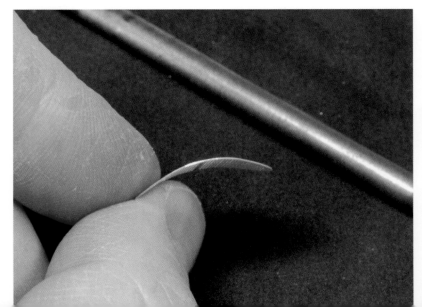

Regularly check the profile being formed against the loco's roof. If the curve is too extreme, place the part on a hard flat surface and gently press the middle downwards to straighten it out a little.

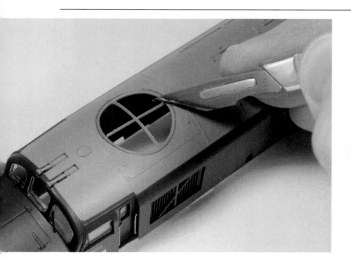

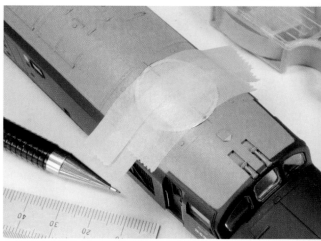

On the Bachmann 37, the moulded surround can be retained as a base for the new roof grille, having removed the cross bracing and scraped away any raised bolt detail.

Mark the centre line of the roof and this will help you align the new grille properly, matching it up with the cross-bracing. Apply some slow-setting superglue or epoxy and fix in place, clamping with masking tape until set. If the grille is to be built up from two layers then repeat the same process, although fixing the overlay is usually a mite trickier, as any excess glue will clog up the beautiful etched mesh beneath; use only the minimum adhesive, applied with a sharp cocktail stick and clamp with tape again.

tant. However, for a job such as this, it should not be more than about 12mm. I use a 6mm diameter rod of mild steel, obtained as the loose-fitting handle of a reaming tool and I've also used the plain shaft of a drill bit to good effect.

Test for a good fit against the roof and repeat the process if the profile is too shallow. Conversely, if the part has gone too far in the other direction, place it upon a hard flat surface and gently press the centre downwards. There will be an element of springiness to it, but it should straighten out slightly. Check against the roof again and repeat until a close fit is gained. Once glue has been applied, press into place and lightly clamp with masking tape. If the model has a compound radius to the roof, the amount of curve can be increased or decreased by judicious use of pressure on the rolling tool.

The etched fan itself may be given a coat of red oxide aerosol primer and the fins bent to form the right sort of pitch. Some way of supporting the new fan has to devised, such as a length of wire suspended from the roof either side of the grille; alternatively, re-fit the original moulded unit.

REGION-SPECIFIC FITTINGS

Diesel locomotives originally built for use on the old Western Region of BR were equipped with different pattern lamp brackets to suit the old Great Western style of oil hand-lamps; a typical facet of the maverick 'Western' mentality. Nearly all plastic lamp-brackets fitted to models are inferior to brass equivalents, both in terms of profile and thickness, and the distinctive WR-style protuberances tend to accentuate this. Etched alternatives are offered by various suppliers and the pack featured here is one of Shawplan's finest. (*See* right.)

A dash of DIY detailing is also involved in this project, in the form of adding a pair of smaller brackets above each headcode panel. These adorned a good many WR 37s and their purpose was to hold a detachable metal bar fitted with a single spotlight. The light was required to be carried when working along certain remote stretches of line, especially in Central and South Wales, with un-gated level crossings. Following careful measuring and marking of the locations, some tiny strips of plastic and wire produced the desired shapes.

Incidentally, the prototype for this model, D6826, may have been sent new to Cardiff Canton shed in 1963 but had, three years later, been resettled at York and was to spend the next fifteen years in the North East and Yorkshire. As I intended to portray this model in the mid-sixties, I removed the blue WR route availability dots printed underneath the engine's numbers

This Shawplan pack of Western Region pattern lamp irons provides enough brackets for three engines and mounting holes require to be drilled. Above the headcode panel are small pieces of 0.020in (0.5mm) square plastic strip and 0.3mm diameter (30SWG) wire to represent a set of brackets for detachable headlights fitted to some WR 37s.

using the T-Cut method, as well as adding some appropriate overhead warning flashes.

This handful of projects has involved a range of different skills, concentrating on cutting away only a small amount of unwanted detail or equipment before adding superior or alternative components. Nevertheless, each of the featured models has only been modified to a relatively small extent and, in the following chapter, we'll consider some slightly more complex techniques and undertakings.

The finished model: other alterations undertaken include a correction to the yellow warning panel that should not continue over the tail-light fittings, instead wrapping around the curved fairings, plus the addition of a single overhead warning symbol on the right of the nose.

CHAPTER 7

Going a Little Further

There are plenty of diesel and electric locomotive models currently being marketed that date back to the 1980s – some go even further back – way before the move to 'high specification' production. As an example, a quick flick through the 2008 Hornby catalogue shows a number of models that, despite now featuring better motors and standards of finish, still lag behind the ultrahigh standards that the same firm is setting with its more recent developments.

If you asked me to list the particular models, I'd list Classes 35, 59, 66, 73 and 86 as prime fodder for the detailer's art, at least until the Margate Company weave their magic and revise these products to match their 31, 50, 56 and others. It's not appropriate to solely highlight Hornby here, as none of Heljan's models feature any etched grilles or other such embellishments. As a result, there is often the need to take a drill, saw, knife and files to the bodyshell and/ or chassis in order to turn a model into a scale reproduction of a real locomotive.

HANDRAILS (REPRISE)

Most of the locomotives mentioned above are former Lima products that now form part of the Hornby family and, although sentimentality can sometimes cloud one's opinions, I can't help but remain partial to certain Lima models that have been around since I was a child. This is despite some of them now having been superseded by newer releases from other makers. Moreover, there are many modellers who insist that certain Lima mouldings can still hold their own against

these new products, especially after super-detailing; the Class 40 being one such example.

I've not been able to bring myself to retire all of my Lima 47s and, once detailed, they can still look OK. Cut away the handrails gradually, working until flush with the surface, using a sharp, flat blade and ending with a scraping action to ensure all material is removed. Remove any scratches with 1,000grade wet/dry paper used damp.

The lamented Italian firm was, however, synonymous with moulded handrails and the number of models that featured separate components was in the minority, even right up to Lima's demise in 2003. Although the removal of unwanted plastic is not difficult, the process does leave large gaps in the paintwork that can be awkward to disguise. Patch-painting, if done thoughtfully enough and with a little judicious weathering, is an option but this also depends on what other detailing tasks are envisaged. Another annoying Lima trait was its habit of

employing a 'one size fits all' policy to many of their locomotive bodyshells and a good example of this is the fitting of modern, square headlight units moulded on to the front of all Class 47s, regardless of their intended period. Hacking this away, filling the accompanying hole and tidying up takes away most of the paint in this area, although being on the cab front means that only the warning panel needs repainting. Indeed, on the featured model, I took the opportunity to add a full yellow panel, as was worn by many 47s during the late-sixties and into the seventies.

Measure and mark out the locations of each new handrail and make small indentations with the point of a sharp scribing tool before drilling holes to suit the gauge of wire to be used. As I use 0.33mm wire, a 0.4mm drill bit was chosen. The hole left by the removal of the modern headlamp moulding requires filling.

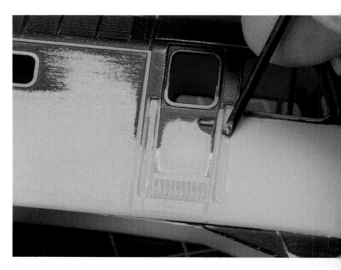

Cutting away the cabside handrails is not so easy, as they're set in a narrow recess. Sharpen the edge of a small, flat blade screwdriver on a grinder or oilstone and this can then be drawn over the surface to act as a scraper.

Due to the amount of excess moulding being cut away, the front ends needed a lot of paintwork reinstating. A minor cheat was to opt for the full yellow warning panel variant to the two-tone green livery, as applied from the late-1960s. The rest of the model was masked-off and the ends primed and painted, before the whole was given a unifying coating of matt varnish.

FILLERS

Model fillers and putties will become important tools to have at hand as more advanced projects are tackled and, along with the dizzying array of adhesive products out there, filling putties also come in many different guises and can suit very distinct applications.

The Milliput range of two-part epoxy putty has been a staple of model-makers for years and packs can be picked up in most hardware stores. The necessary mixing and slow curing time can be a little annoying but it can be used for filling deep holes in one shot and will take being drilled into; something that many other products can only claim to be up to. Milliput can also be sculpted and used for other purposes, such as mould-making, and will adhere to almost anything.

Humbrol's Model Filler is an interesting product, being a low-viscosity liquid that is suited to plastics only. The solution works to melt the plastic and, thus, blend-in any blemishes or small gaps. Repeated thin applications can deal with larger gaps but with the risk of softening the plastic too much. Aimed largely at plastic kit building, it does still have the odd use on locomotive projects such as filling scratches.

Knifing Putty is sold through automotive accessory stores and is designed for filling small indentations in car paintwork. Thus, it can only be used for shallow recesses, although it sets quickly and can be abraded to a very smooth finish. Other auto fillers may also be helpful, not least as their rapid curing times are welcome, although relatively high cost is a point against them. The American firm Squadron Products produce modelling putty under the banner of MMD. This combines most of the advantages mentioned above, such as rapid setting, no need for pre-mixing and a fine finish, and is well-priced. I picked up my tube from the Ian Allan transport bookshop near Waterloo Station, London.

All of the products mentioned are formulated to allow filing or sanding to a good finish and using filling products is similar to applying Polyfilla when decorating, only on a much smaller scale. As an example, in order to fill the hole left by the removal of the square headlamp on the Lima Class 47, a small scrap of plastic card was glued behind the hole and some model putty applied into the aperture, leaving it proud of the surface until hardened completely. The filler can then be rubbed down to a flush surface using fine abrasive paper.

There's a wide range of model fillers and putties. Epoxy putties such as Milliput are two-pack formulas that require mixing together before use and can, therefore, be more time-consuming; while others, such as MMD's fast drying white putty, are more convenient but not as strong. Each product has its own advantages and disadvantages and it's a question of choosing the most appropriate for each situation.

Glazing

All locomotives have windows of one sort or another so, sooner or later, we have to deal with replacement, repair or even removal of some areas of glazing. Happily, virtually every new model produced by Hornby, Bachmann and Heljan over the last decade has come with good quality, flush-fitting windows. Even Lima scored some triumphs in the glazing department before their demise, although the integrally moulded wipers could be a little frustrating, such as on the Class 73.

A novel production method was employed by Hornby when it introduced a model of the BR Class 58 in 1982. The demountable cab mouldings are formed from single blocks of a clear plastic and this is masked carefully when the livery is applied and, thus, provides glazing that is as lifelike as anything offered since. Wipers are also moulded into the same unit but, unlike some of Lima's efforts in this respect, these look splendid. A drawback of the one-piece moulding arises when purchasing a model with a factory-applied weathering finish, most of which can be rather heavy handed. The unwanted brown spray can be removed to an extent but I've yet to find a 100 per cent satisfactory method for this so, take my advice and buy a model with a pristine finish.

The Hornby Class 58 uses a single block of clear plastic to form the cab mouldings. Having used a factory-weathered model as the basis of my detailing project, the windows were covered in 'dirt', while I wanted them to be clean enough to show off the detailed interior. A tiny amount of T-Cut was rubbed into each panel with a cotton bud, followed by the use of an ultra-soft buffing mop in a mini drill set to a low speed.

Great care must be exercised with the powered mop, applying only the lightest pressure for just a second at a time to prevent the plastic from overheating. Although not a perfect remedy, it's the only way to remove the factory-applied 'dirt' without ruining the clear glazing.

A more subtle weathering job adorns this super-detailed 58 and the interior can now be seen through the windows.

For more 'senior' models, South Eastern Finecast have been in the business of producing bespoke flushglazing packs for r-t-r models for some time and its range is certainly comprehensive. Vacuum-formed in clear plastic, the individual windows need only be cut with a pair of scissors and carefully glued into their respective apertures. A little fettling may be required, particularly if a model has been refinished and the openings have received a few extra layers of paint. These packs are inexpensive and provide, in the main, good results.

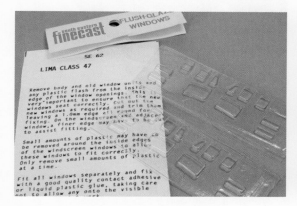

South Eastern Finecast has long held the monopoly on vacuum-formed locomotive flushglazing kits. These are readily available, inexpensive ways of improving older models and packs cater for virtually all r-t-r releases that do not already have flush-fitting windows. Fitting instructions are supplied with every pack.

Most models do not require any modifications to accept the flushglazing, although some apertures may need a little fettling with needle files. Cut out the individual windows and push into place. Use of a clear-setting adhesive is paramount in case of spills or smudges, Deluxe's Glue 'n' Glaze being ideal.

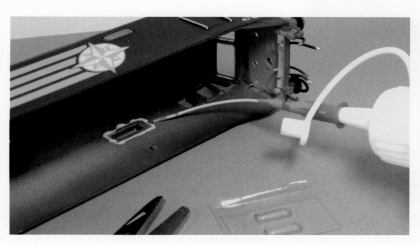

Using a Micro Tip and delivery tube from the Deluxe applicator range, the Glue 'n' Glaze can be delivered in a controlled way to the window surround. Keep it well away from the aperture and cut the glazing with plenty of waste wherever possible to achieve a larger bonding surface. Allow to set completely before reassembly.

There are, however, a few gaps in the flushglaze range and this presents us with having to produce our own 'glass', either by using clear plastic sheet cut to size or by making use of clear liquid formulas that are excellent for smaller apertures, where there is little risk of being damaged by repeated handling. Hand-made glazing is probably the most impressive-looking, if the panels are fitted well and without glue spillage.

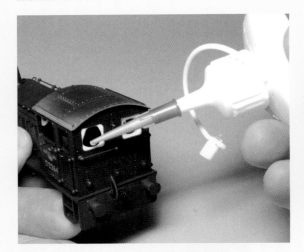

Where flushglaze packs are not available, the Glue 'n' Glaze can be used in its own right as a glazing medium. Apply around the inside of an aperture, using a Micro Tip applicator.

Then take a clean cocktail stick and draw the fluid across the opening to form a film, taking care not to introduce any air bubbles. Set the model aside in a dust-free environment to dry and the fluid will set absolutely clear.

The Glue 'n' Glaze may not cope with larger orifices, so making your own glazing from clear plastic sheet is an alternative. Carefully measure the window and transfer the dimensions to the plastic, cutting out with a fresh blade and testing for a good, close fit. Use a fine needle file to make any adjustments and to form any curved corners. Again, the Glue 'n' Glaze can be used to fix the clear panels in place.

An alternative adhesive, for those in a rush, is an odourless superglue in the Roket range (again by Deluxe) and a miniscule amount of this, carefully applied, will fix the windows fast within seconds, without any of the side-effects common with other superglues and clear plastic.

DIGGING A HOLE

Replacing small or large moulded grilles with etched substitutes requires some seemingly drastic action and I've demonstrated some methods here, using a Hornby Class 58. (*See* below.) Heljan's more recent 58 model is certainly attractive but it still lacks etched grilles, so the same procedures could be followed for both products.

After procuring suitable replacements and determining the required aperture sizes, drill out most of the waste with a mini power drill, keeping the tool at least a few millimetres away from the edges. It's important to support the model adequately while doing this, as a slip with the tool may damage the loco and yourself. The perforated plastic may then be cut away with a sturdy blade to leave enough access for a file to work the edges back to the final dimensions. Using a sanding drum in a drill can speed up the process, especially with round openings, but this technique requires a bit of practice to prevent excessive amounts of material disappearing before your eyes. Any raised rims from the now-defunct grilles must also be shaved away in a similar way to how the handrails were ditched on the Lima 47, leaving a nice flat surface for the new components to sit on.

If an etched grille is to replace a moulded representation, a suitable hole should be created. With circular roof grilles, drill a series of 3mm holes within the area to be removed, keeping away from the edges. Hold the model securely whilst drilling, preferably in a vice or pressed firmly against a stable surface to avoid any mishaps.

Cut away most of the waste material, using a sturdy blade to connect the individual holes. Then, use either a round file or a sanding drum in a mini power-drill to work the aperture into the correct shape, ensuring that it does not become oversized. Keep the moulded rim of the former grill in place and use it as a guide, filing it flat once the hole has been finished.

Repeat the process with any side grilles but, if the aperture has square edges, use a broad, flat file to work to the final size. Again, keep the moulded rims as a guide before cutting them away to give a clean, flat surface for the new parts.

Roll the new roof grilles to shape, as demonstrated in the previous chapter, and glue in place. Low-tack masking tape is perfect for clamping the parts in place without the risk of damage as the tape is later removed.

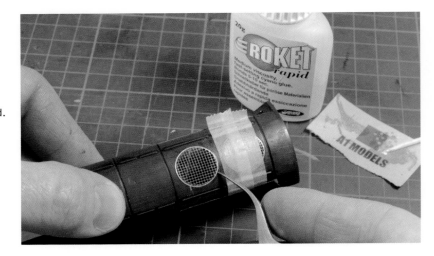

For this Class 58, the A1 Models' side grilles are laminated from two layers, the cross-braced parts sitting below the mesh panels. Ensure each layer is firmly in place before adding the overlays.

Not all parts are like-for-like exchanges, however, and the Hornby model's most notable flaw is the lack of any exhaust stack on the roof. A1 Models have designed an etched brass unit that must be folded to shape and fitted into a hole carved into the central roof panel (all of the etched components fitted here are from the A1 range). Accurate marking-out of this aperture is crucial if the exhaust is to sit well. Mark a centre line along the length of the engine's roof, and do likewise along the brass unit, before folding it to match the irregular hexagon shape of the end piece. Keep the half-etched lines on the inside and use a Hold 'n' Fold, if possible, to ensure that all folds are sharp and avoid any twisting.

The Hornby 58 lacks any representation of the exhaust unit, so this brass substitute must be folded to shape and a suitable aperture created. Its location can be marked by holding it firmly while a pencil or blade transfers the rough shape on to the model.

The final working lines can be refined with the unit removed and, using an engineer's square, ensure that the hole will be straight and perpendicular in relation to the body. Always err on the side of caution, as it's so much easier to make a hole bigger than it is to reduce it. Once certain that all is correct, go through the drilling, cutting and filing routine again, checking for fit regularly

and making any necessary alterations. Once the exhaust is fixed in place (ideally using epoxy), any gaps can be filled in with modelling putty and tidied up ready for undercoating.

Copious amounts of other details were also added to this 58, many of which aren't necessary if working on a Heljan product, such as wire handrails and separate cab front jumper cables to replace the bulky mouldings. By the end, such was the amount of work visited upon the model, preserving the factory finish was out of the question!

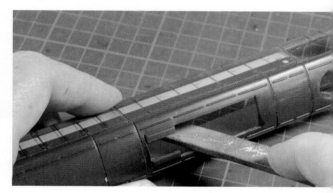

ABOVE: Final dimensions can then be refined before the waste is removed using a drill, knife and files.

BELOW: Any gaps that may result around the new exhaust unit can be plugged with model filler. Other details added include the missing longitudinal ribs cut from 0.020×0.040in (0.5×1.0mm) plastic strip, brass lifting eyes, handrails and engine room door handles.

The amount of added detail can be appreciated here, either replacing heavily moulded features or instating missing equipment. In addition to the grilles and exhaust unit, plenty of other A1 Models' etched components are available for the Class 58, including sandboxes and bodyside guards (fitted alongside the cab doors). Small extras, such as the bogie pipe runs, sand fillers and bufferbeam footsteps have all been improvised from wire, strip brass and plastic.

ENTER THE SOLDERING IRON

Further to the earlier notes on miniature snow-ploughs, if you are now becoming more familiar with folding brass components to shape, then swapping a moulded plastic set of ploughs for some finer etched blades will make for a superior level of finish. Various packs are available and most are provided with half-etched fold lines, enabling the distinctive profile of the blades to be formed. However, it seems to be common for all packs not to provide either integrated or separate mounting brackets, manufacturers suggesting using brass wire to form some suitable mounts.

The centre blades of the A1 Models' pack, once folded, require help to keep their shape. Glue is an option, but mastering a bit of basic soldering wouldn't go amiss. Let's start with some basics:

two pieces of metal need to be heated to a sufficient degree to allow a third material – the solder – to melt and flow between the two metals and, as everything cools, the solder hardens and forms a very strong bond. The solder will only adhere to surfaces if they are free from grease or other residues that may remain from the etching process, so the first thing to do is to clean all surfaces with abrasive paper or a fibreglass scratch brush.

While this is happening, a soldering iron can be warming in its stand and, as the tip gets up to temperature, it should be drawn over a clean, moist sponge to remove any contaminants. For small items such as these snowploughs, it's often a good idea to 'tin' both parts of each joint with a little solder before actually joining them. Decide where the joints will be and apply a small blob of solder to the hot iron tip and place it on to the brass. As the metal warms, the molten solder will

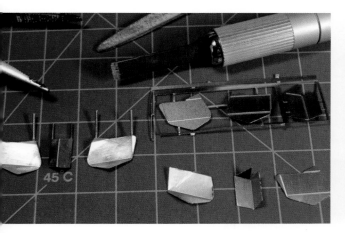

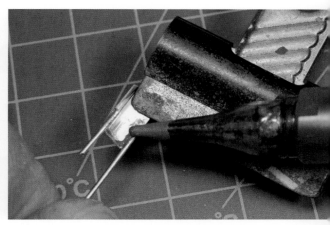

A good set of etched miniature snowploughs are hard to beat and this A1 Models' set makes up into an accurate representation of the real things. After cutting from the fret and trimming, the separate components must be folded to shape, the half-etched fold lines remaining on the inside (unseen) face. No form of mounting bracket is provided so some lengths of brass wire should be pressed into service.

With the blade held in a clamp or vice, a length of 0.9mm stiff brass wire is fixed to the rear corners. Epoxy glue will work, but a decent soldered joint will be more resilient. Lightly 'tin' the two parts with a drop of solder before marrying them together, adding a drop of flux before applying the hot iron and this will help the solder to flood into the joint.

drift from the iron to the work piece. Remove the heat and let the solder cool, then clean the iron's tip again.

Bring the two parts together and clamp, if possible. Then introduce a small amount of liquid or paste flux to the joint and, again with a small drop of solder on the tip, apply to the joint and wait for the flux to transfer the solder into and around the joint, repeating with more solder if necessary. Once cooled, the joint should be nice and strong and any remaining traces of flux must be removed by washing with detergent and an old toothbrush. This level of cleanliness should be adopted as a matter of course, as failure to remove the acid-rich flux will result in future corrosion of the joint.

For the snowplough brackets, each length of 0.9mm wire was soldered in place before trimming to provide something to hold whilst jointing. The photographs show my fingers holding the wire but I'd rather you clamped both parts as best as possible – repeated soldering has led me to develop 'asbestos' fingertips. Brass is chosen for modelling components for many reasons, one of the most pertinent being its excellent heat transferral properties, so be warned!

The new ploughs can be attached to the underside of the bufferbeam, drilling mounting holes for the wire brackets will provide a very firm joint. A coat of primer, followed by a suitable top coat finishes the job.

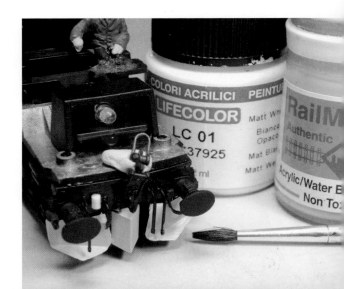

New buffers and snowploughs transform the front 'face' of the Vi-Trains' Class 37.

This is another skill that requires practice in order to build confidence and ability. Small-scale tasks such as this are a perfect introduction.

This more or less covers all of the basic skills involved with detailing work, save for painting and weathering. Now is the time to aim for consolidation of these techniques, which can only be brought about by repetition and through developing an awareness of potential improvement opportunities. Why not try formulating your own project ideas, looking at your model collection, cheap second-hand stuff or by drawing some inspiration from articles in the modelling press? Additionally, just scouting through the catalogues of detailing component makers, such as Shawplan or A1, can often provide food for thought. Remember, that confidence can only grow with familiarity.

The Western Region lamp brackets discussed previously can easily be reproduced as they boast, in most cases, a wholly flat profile. In contrast, the more standard bracket is quite a complex shape to recreate from a flat strip of brass and variations exist, depending on where the component is sited. Shawplan offer a pack of etched-brass strips intended for bending to shape and a small Hold 'n' Fold unit is very useful here. These two small brackets are for mounting to a Class 20.

The new lamp brackets can be seen fixed below the front windows, along with other minor modifications. Wire handrails (0.33mm brass) have replaced the plastic mouldings, small strips of plastic acting as supports. Etched headcode discs replace the over-sized originals, although the attendant mounting clips have had to be cut away and replaced. Brass buffers and etched backing plates are in place, along with new bufferbeam hoses and fine windscreen wipers.

CHAPTER 8

Coupling-Up

As I write this, there is currently much debate, particularly in the so-called 'Finescale' pages, concerning realistic layout operation. Some writers and correspondents have taken issue with the speed at which locomotives deposit their rolling stock in a siding or how they move off, with barely a few seconds being allowed for the act of coupling-up. Personally, I enjoy nothing more than to potter about the sidings with a shunter hooking on or off a few wagons, moving them here and there while mainline trains trundle by. Taking time to represent the clanging of buffers, the connecting of hoses and testing of brakes also fits in with the time it usually takes me to fumble around with the scale couplings on my stock!

It's all down to personal taste, however, and who am I to dictate what people do with their own layouts? Sometimes having a coupling method that works in an instant is considered necessary, not least on far-flung fiddle yards or sidings where manual operation is impossible. Luckily, there are plenty of coupler options for OO-gauge modellers, each offering their own advantages and drawbacks.

TENSION LOCKS AND THE NEM SAGA

The well-known 'tension lock' system of couplings dates back nearly five decades, to the

The erstwhile tension-lock couplings, as fitted to British-outline model railways since pioneered by Tri-ang in the 1960s, are about as far from the prototype as possible. At least they have been reduced in size over the past decade (left).

days of Tri-ang. Funnily enough, the state of play in the 1960s was that few brands of model railways offered compatible couplings. When the formerly competing Tri-ang and Hornby Dublo both ended up being owned by the same company, in 1964, it became apparent that some sort of standardization was needed to promote the sales of stocks of both brands.

The solution was to produce a series of 'converter' wagons with the Hornby Dublo coupler type at one end and Tri-ang's at the other. This was only a temporary measure, as the sideways-acting Hornby Dublo unit soon disappeared in favour of the Tri-ang tension lock that is still with us today. Although it has been refined over the decades, it still works on the same principle of the hooks locking into the loop of the following vehicle when under pulling force (i.e. tension). However, the vertical tails can be raised by using sprung ramps between the rails and, once the tension in the coupling is released, the hooks lift and the vehicles part. These uncouplers can be unsightly unless well disguised and the modern, narrow version of the tension lock can actually be less reliable in such instances, as it has a tendency to 'miss' the ramps.

I used the term 'funnily enough' above because, even after all this time, there is still no definite harmonization of couplings across the board. The NEM coupling pocket (meaning that the couplings comply with the Normen Europäischer Modellbahnen set of European standards for model railways) has been an attempt to rectify this lack of standardization but coupling heights can differ wildly, even within a single product range, never mind between manufacturers. It is, however, a starting point, and the humble tension locks are now easily replaceable on most new models, simply snapping into NEM pockets. Some models, mostly of rolling stock, include alternative couplers within the packaging and are easily interchanged. Furthermore, advances in close-coupling equipment have led to Hornby fitting their locomotives with similar systems to compliment its rolling stock.

The interchangeable nature of the NEM pocket means that all manner of different couplings can be tried, all simply clipping into place. European patterns, such as Roco or 'hook and loop' types, can be used if desired, although these can look just as out of place on the front of a locomotive as the tension lock, and some are more difficult to disengage without resorting to the 'great hand from the sky' trick. They are, however, ideal for use within rakes of rolling stock or between multiple unit cars.

Another relatively recent development for British r-t-r stock has been the provision of NEM coupling pockets that allow for quick and easy interchanging of coupler units. However, these are still far from standard kit in terms of fitment and coupling height.

The NEM pockets permit the use of many different couplers, such as these Roco units, now available as separate accessories from Hornby. They may look unusual when fitted to a locomotive but, if utilized in fixed rakes of stock, provide reliable running and reasonably close coupling.

A very popular alternative coupling is the Kadee range of automatic, buck-eye style units, as fitted to overseas and, increasingly, to modern British freight stock. Many sizes are available along with a choice of mountings, including NEM-friendly types.

KADEES

Developed for use on 'HO'-scale American-outline stock, Kadee couplers have become popular worldwide, due largely to their reliable performance and ease of fitting. In Britain, they may not be prototypical for all but the General Motors-built Class 66 or 67 locomotives, but they are reasonably close in appearance to the buckeye couplings fitted to Southern Region Classes 33/1 and 73, along with BR coaching stock and electric multiple units. Even some steam locomotives sported a form of buckeye, namely the corridor-fitted tenders of LNER A3s and A4s. However, seeing them used willy-nilly on things like Great Western 'Castles' or LMS 'Jubilees' does not agree with my aesthetic sensibilities!

The benefits of fitting and using the Kadee system are numerous. Firstly, coupling and uncoupling is simple and can be controlled by hand-held or hidden magnets. Secondly, there is minimal separation distance between vehicles, whether the train is being pushed or pulled. This is in contrast to tension locks with which, upon coupling-up, the stock can sit quite close together but, once under way, the gaps between

vehicles open up drastically. Thirdly, the 'knuckles' themselves come pre-built, leaving only those packs supplied with draft boxes requiring assembly. Finally, the vast range of sizes available, plus the back-up of many different accessories, makes them a very attractive option.

The prescribed working height for all Kadees is 25/64in (9.9mm) from the top of the rails to the centre of the 'knuckle'. The array of possible units to fit include long, medium or short shanks, all in either under- or over-set form, along with an added choice of fitting in an upward or inverted draft box. All this presents an unparalleled range of height adjustments, increased further by the addition of shims, if necessary. Perhaps the easiest to fit are the NEM pocket-mounting versions that are available in a choice of four shank lengths (Nos 17–20). Choosing a length depends on the stock in question and the tightness of curves on your layout. Illustrated above and overleaf is a pair of Bachmann Class 20s coupled with No.19 Kadees and, as can be seen, the long shanks are necessary to prevent the buffers from 'locking' on corners. Being American-designed, Kadees are obviously intended for locomotives and rolling stock without buffers, so we British modellers are bound to lose out on the true

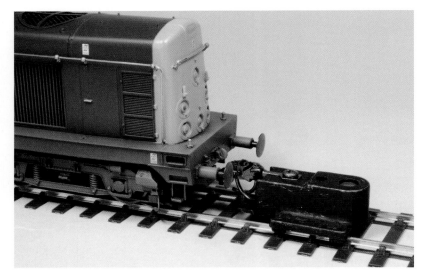

As with all coupling units, achieving a consistent height is paramount for reliable use. Kadee produce a handy height gauge that clips on to a piece of track and allows instant checking of couplings.

One of the great advantages of the Kadee system is the realistic close coupling. However, they were never designed for use with buffer-fitted stock and this can lead to problems when traversing curves where the buffers can lock together. Therefore, the couplings must be set to protrude far enough from the bufferbeam to give adequate clearance, thus losing some of the close coupling advantage.

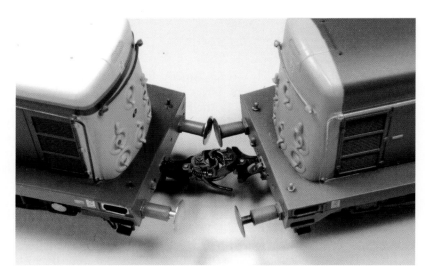

close-coupling permitted by this system. Having sideways movement in the 'knuckles' gives more leeway and the draft-box Kadees have this facility. As for the NEM-mounted units, lateral play is dictated by the mount itself, usually located on a bogie frame.

Automatic magnetic uncoupling is achieved by the drop wires being forced apart and, thus, opening up the 'knuckles'. The same performance is offered as with the humble tension lock, in that the uncoupling magnet can be passed, even at a slow speed, without the couplings opening, unless the tension in the joint is released i.e. the train having stopped. A delayed action is also possible where a train comes to a halt over a magnet: the tension is released and the 'knuckles' open up. The train can then be propelled away from the magnet, yet the knuckles will remain open until the pressure is released once again. In this case, the wagon can be deposited at any point along the line, reducing the number of magnets needed.

Where NEM-type Kadees can't be used, a set of draft boxes must be constructed. These can be assembled in a variety of ways to suit each project and the supplied instructions are extensive and well illustrated. Once the coupling has been fitted to the draft box, a spring is added to allow the coupling to turn in its slot but will always return to the centre position.

The fully assembled Kadee (No.38 medium straight shank) with draft box, set up with an inverted mounting for fitting to a Bachmann Class 66.

Although the Bachmann Class 66 comes with NEM pockets, using them means having to forego fitting the bufferbeam valances. Instead, fit a draft box-mounted Kadee, modifying the bogie frames slightly to suit. After unclipping them from the main frames and carefully cutting away the NEM pockets, plus a bit more material from the fronts of the bogie frames. Be sure to leave enough plastic to allow the frame to be clipped back into place.

Some shims of plastic card are needed to bring the coupling and its mounting box to the correct height. Trial and error, checking against the Kadee height gauge, is the way to go, using double-sided tape instead of glue. I needed about 4.5mm to 'jack up' the mount on this 66.

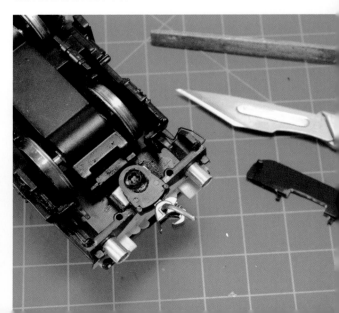

Once satisfied that the coupling is set at the right height and that it works properly, it can be secured in place permanently and the valance fitted, having had an area cut out to allow the coupling to protrude. Although mounted below the traditional draw-hook, as opposed to sitting alongside as it does on the prototype, the Kadee sits well on this EWS Class 66.

Bachmann have recently been offering some of its modern r-t-r freight rolling stock with Eazi Mate knuckle couplings. These look a little similar to – and are compatible with – Kadee units. Unfortunately, they are not always set at the 'standard' specified Kadee operating height, requiring some adjustment.

SCALE COUPLINGS

For the purist, there's nothing as prototypical as a working screw coupling dangling from the front of a locomotive. Dummy units, of varying quality, are supplied with most model engines these days but these should only be used for purely cosmetic purposes. Working scale-couplings consist of only a few working parts and mirror the operation of the real thing: a drawhook, spring and split pin form the main part, accompanied by either a screw-adjusted or three-link chain, depending on prototype. By and large, three-links are confined to the older, smaller shunting classes or steam-era traction used on loose-coupled freight workings. The screw-adjusting links allowed for slack to be taken-up to prevent shocks and strains that could result in breakage.

Depending on the brand of coupling, they may be supplied ready-assembled or in pieces, the building of which can be a little tedious. A pair of round-nose pliers is useful in shaping the chain links to an even, round shape and they should be closed tightly to prevent failure

in use. There are even some working miniature screw-couplings on the market, but it's not really a practical option to have the coupling set too tightly. Indeed, I always couple up to my locomotives using the wagons' links, as these are usually slightly longer and more flexible, allowing more slack when corners are encountered.

Being able to fit a working screw coupling depends on the amount of space available behind the bufferbeam. Consisting of a draw-hook, spring and split pin, the coupling itself may come ready assembled (as with this Romford set) or will require putting together. Either the draw-hook or mounting hole may need fettling to gain a nice, slightly loose fit.

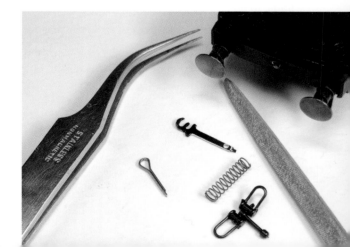

When fitting a new drawhook to a ready-to-run engine, a moulded hook will probably need to be cut away first and a new hole drilled. As the slot is a narrow one, it's best to drill two or three small holes in a vertical line before linking them with a sharp, pointed blade. This is fine if the bufferbeam is moulded plastic, although cast steel is increasingly being employed for entire chassis units and this is certainly more difficult to work with. Fine engineer's broaches will enlarge an existing or drilled hole, although, in some cases, I find it quicker to fettle the drawhook to fit the existing hole. This isn't always practical, as a minimum of material needs to be retained around the split pin-hole.

If working on the Hornby Class 56, for instance, the front panel of the chassis must be lifted, by undoing four small screws, to allow the swivelling NEM pocket to be removed. With the draw-hook passed through the bufferbeam, the spring is inserted and squeezed slightly while the split pin is pushed through the hole in the hook and the tails bent outwards to keep it in place.

The use of a sprung drawhook is essential for reliable running and to prevent constant derailments, particularly on curved track; the springs allow the couplings to slacken a little and will also absorb any jolts. Naturally, such springs should be fitted to each item of rolling stock, as well as to the locomotive. Unfortunately, fitting sprung drawhooks to some models can be a near-hopeless task, as witnessed with Bachmann's

Class 20, which hosts a fixing screw directly behind the centre of the bufferbeam, running into the cast-steel chassis. Being faced with hacking a large recess in the metal chassis, and then having to determine how to re-fix the body, left me feeling faint. Instead, I took the lazy route and compromised with a fixed hook, albeit one that protruded a few millimetres more than usual, in an effort to give a little more slack in the coupling. In service, I've yet to experience any problems with this machine, although it doesn't run over any particularly tight corners and I always ensure that a wagon with an especially loose coupling is marshalled immediately behind to compensate: not an ideal solution by any means but it does work.

One of the main drawbacks of using scale couplings is the lack of any automatic coupling or uncoupling. The delicate nature of the links, and the restricted space between vehicles, makes coupling a tricky business. This limitation also dictates that any shunting manoeuvres have to take place on a readily-accessible part of a layout and the constant leaning-over may put a lot of people off. Another negative aspect is that they are simply not suited to layouts with any degree of tight curves, as the couplings cannot cope with being stretched. Buffer-locking and strained couplings both equate to derailments

With other models, something can get in the way of a working draw-hook. Bachmann's Class 20 has the body fixing screw placed directly behind the bufferbeam and, with the chassis being a solid block of metal, performing any sort of surgery is difficult.

A possible compromise to overcome this problem is to fit a fixed draw-hook and rely on the springing of the rolling stock's couplings to absorb any jolts. Here, an etched hook from the Mainly Trains range (ref. MT356) has been fixed firmly into a shallow hole in the bufferbeam with epoxy glue. By ensuring that the hook protrudes enough to give the couplings plenty of slack, the train should be able to cope with gentle curves without derailing. In any case, scale couplings should not be used on layouts with sharp corners and pointwork.

and frustration. Incidentally, an effective home-made coupling tool consists of a long piece of fine, stiff wire with a hook at one end, preferably magnetized to pick up the links. In addition, fixing this tool to the end of a miniature pen-shaped torch will improve visibility.

THE KEEN SYSTEM

If you tend to keep your trains in a fixed formation, then the Keen close coupling system may be just up your street. According to the sales blurb, this system is 'designed to permit r-t-r and kit-built OO coaching stock to run buffer-to-buffer and still cope with Hornby radius one curves'. This is indeed a bold statement but, after experimenting with it myself I can say that, if the equipment is fitted properly, it's true.

The couplings work to keep vehicles close together on straight track until a curve is encountered; then the cars are pushed apart and the gap increases as the curve tightens, allowing the bend to be traversed without the stock fouling each other. This same principle is now used on many r-t-r carriage models released during the past decade, following on from what has been used on overseas models for much longer. Unlike on

these products, however, the Keen system does not come equipped with a self-centred spring arrangement, although I've not found this to be a problem.

The units can be fitted to almost any carriage and many locomotives, just as long as there is enough room behind the bufferbeams. Some older Hornby products, like the Class 37, 47 or 25, would need some serious modification, as the bogies on these models are retained at the ends rather than pivoting in the centre, as with most Lima offerings. Although, with the latter, at least the non-powered bogies have a central bolster that leaves the underside of the chassis free. Roger Keen provides some indications of what is and what is not possible with this system on his website and promotional material so, if you're interested, contact details are included in the Appendix.

Whatever stock is being fitted it's vital, just as with all such couplings, that each unit is set to a consistent height. Although the instructions state a desired height from the rails for the couplings, some margin for compromise is available to suit the vagaries of the models in question, as long as they are standardized with each other and are kept in their fixed formations. There is scope

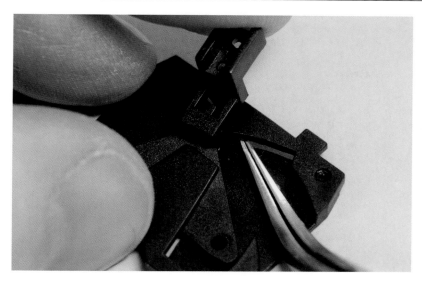

The Keen Systems' coupling mount needs to fit well inside the base to allow free movement but without too much slack. Carefully trim any excess material from the retaining pin before fitting into the coupling base; lever the front edge upwards to give the mount a little more room to slot into place.

The Keen mounts allow for any coupling type to be fitted and a range of options are available from the same supplier. Alternatively, NEM type units will fit, including NEM Kadees.

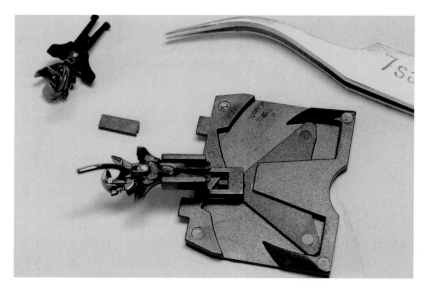

for adjusting coupling height, either in how the base plate is fitted in the first instance, or by adding plastic shims into the coupling box, if the coupling needs to be lowered.

While fitting this system to a Lima HST set, the coupling base was fitted to the non-motorized power car with little fuss, sitting happily on to the underside of the chassis with no surgery required. Only the moulded air tanks had to be unclipped, trimmed and then re-fixed on top of the new addition, ensuring that it did not interfere with the moving parts. Note that part of the rear tank may need a central area cutting out to give the coupling mount room to move from side to side, but this depends on the radius of curves on your layout. Luckily, I didn't need to worry about this as my HST will be used on an end-to-end layout, with only very gentle curves on the main line, and it's unlikely to be sent into any of the goods loops or sidings!

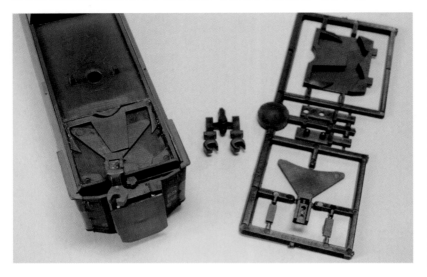

When fitting the system to a rake of Mark 3 cars, a square hole needs to be cut in the floor. Mark out the size of the base, drill a series of holes within the lines and then cut away the waste with a sturdy blade. Carefully use a flat file to work back to the final dimensions, test-fitting the base as you go. Aim for a nice tight fit and fix in place with epoxy. It may be necessary to add some reinforcing plastic strips on the inside and check that the base is level and true before the glue sets.

On this Lima HST power car, the coupling base sits on the floor of the chassis, while the air tanks can be refitted to disguise the unit. The coupler mount box has been trimmed back to permit very close coupling on this buffer-less formation.

The Keen Systems' coupling units really come into their own when fitted to something like a HST set. As neither the power cars nor the Mark 3 stock feature buffers, ultra-close coupling is possible. When running straight, the carriages are only a fraction of a millimetre apart, yet when a curve is encountered, the couplings act to push the vehicles apart. A range of working gangway connectors is also produced by Keen.

The motorized power car, on the other hand, threw up a problem, as the motor bogie takes up much more space and the underframe moulding flares out to retain the bogie. This means that either the coupling base must be modified or the bogie mount changed. Neither is particularly straightforward but I addressed the problem by modifying the motor bogie. Namely, I cut away the retaining mouldings of the chassis and the corresponding 'wings' of the bogie frame, built up the inside of the car's roof with plastic card and used some cutting-edge engineering (a press stud) to attach and pivot the motor. This left the chassis free to be modified by the fitting of the Keen coupling base. Not exactly rocket science, I know, but it's effective and allows the bogie to rotate freely and also to pivot laterally, just as it did before.

None of this need worry those intending to buy a couple of Hornby's completely new HST power cars that were nearing release while I finished this book. As with all of Hornby's new-generation D&E era models, a sliding coupling mount comes fitted to the gangway ends, permitting close coupling. However, the Margate-based firm have yet to announce any plans to revamp the range of Mark3 stock, so the Keen system still has its uses in this instance.

SPRATT AND WINKLE

Endorsed as a 'finescale' product, the Spratt and Winkle is the perfect compromise between automatic operation and scale appearance. If fiddling about with screw or three-link couplings is not appealing, then this system offers an unobtrusive and near-prototypical appearance with remote magnetic operation.

Helpfully, trial packs are offered at a very reasonable price and this allows the system to be assessed without too much commitment. The trial packs consist of enough components to equip four vehicles and full, illustrated instructions are supplied. Couplings consist of an etched brass hook attached to a 'paddle', pivoting on a separate brass base. A fine-wire loop is fitted at each end and this, in conjunction with the dual-acting hook, provides a suitable pushing and pulling interface, taking the point of contact away from the buffers and removing the risk of wagons 'locking-up' on curves or pointwork. The hooks also feature a mounting for cosmetic three-link couplings to dangle from the buffer-beam, which looks very realistic, especially when viewed from a modest distance. Locomotives only require the wire loops to be fitted at the bufferbeam and this does not interfere with the full addition of brake pipes, hoses and dummy screw couplings.

An unobtrusive and finescale-standard method of automatic coupling is the Spratt and Winkle. Available in inexpensive trial packs, it consists of etched-brass hooks and mounting bases, plus various gauges of wire. Operation is with the use of hidden magnets beneath the track.

Relying on hidden magnets placed between the rails, they act on a similar principle to other magnetically operated couplings in that once a magnet is encountered, the hooks are drawn towards it. Suitable magnets are supplied and these can be located wherever desired, such as at the entrance to a siding. The train is brought to a stop over the magnet and then eased back slightly to compress the couplings. The hooks drop and the train can then be moved away, leaving the wagon behind. Another feature is 'delayed' uncoupling, where the same procedure is followed but, instead of drawing away, the train is then propelled further into the siding with the wagon remaining uncoupled, just as is possible with Kadee couplings.

First attempts at fitting this system may take a little time to get right, but once a few vehicles have been fitted, the technique soon becomes familiar. Keeping all couplings to a uniform height is imperative and it's worth constructing a simple height-gauge to help during fitting. Alternatively, keep a specific wagon as a 'master' to test others against. It's worth mentioning that the Spratt and Winkle has been designed prima-rily for use with locomotives and freight wagons (especially four-wheel vehicles), but there's no reason why it can't be used on most other stock, including bogie carriages. For the full benefits of the system to be enjoyed, the makers recommend a minimum of 3ft (915mm) radius curves although, if the train is being pulled only and not pushing in delayed coupling mode, then 2ft (610mm) curves can be negotiated.

There is certainly plenty of choice in terms of coupling types and systems out there, either ready-fitted, available as drop-in replacements, or kits. Each is suited to various operating styles and track specifications, and choice is purely down to the modeller. Indeed, standardizing on a single type is far from essential. Passenger rakes could be semi-permanently fixed with close-coupling units and engines and 'local' freight traffic fitted with a suitable automatic format for ease of shunting, while modern freight stock could utilize the Kadee pattern to mimic the growing use of knuckle couplers. It could be argued that such diversity is entirely prototypical, as there is far from a standard coupling on today's hi-tech railway.

The dual-acting coupling hooks act to pull and push the vehicles, preventing buffer locking on corners. These are not as difficult to assemble and fit as they may at first seem.

CHAPTER 9

Think Electric

An early model railway ambition of mine was to produce an extensive layout based on the West Coast Main Line (WCML) scene of the late-1980s. I remember being captivated by an article in *Railway Modeller* that featured a OO-gauge layout called 'Carstairs Junction'. This model, although not of a real location, certainly caught the flavour of the WCML in a period when I was an active 'spotter'. Only recently, after looking through some old magazines, did I realize that the layout boasted no catenary wire strung between the scratch-built masts; but I can still see how it had transfixed me at the time.

Despite a surprisingly large range of ready-to-run electric locomotives being available, not many layout builders feature the electrified railway. Perhaps it's the extra work involved in erecting a system of overhead wires or laying yards of third rail and other equipment that puts people off. There's yet to be a realistic – and easy to fit – mass-produced OO-gauge catenary system, although I'm sure this will change in the coming years.

Hornby offer Classes 86, 90, 91 and 92 in its range, plus the soon-to-be re-released ex-Lima Class 87, as well as Pendolino and Eurostar units. There are also some excellent resin kits of earlier 25kV AC locomotives, such as the Class 81 and 85 produced by DC Kits. For third-rail modellers, only the ex-Lima Class 73 and Hornby's dual-voltage Eurostar and Class 92 represent suitable r-t-r models and the 73 is an electro-diesel rather than a pure 750V DC electric.

Naturally, there are some details that are peculiar to electric locomotives and the roof-mounted pantograph is the first component that springs to mind. Both Hornby and Lima offered models with working pantographs (allowing for power collection from a catenary system), although they usually included an unsightly slide switch atop the roof. The Hornby 92 differs in this respect by being fitted with dummy plastic pantographs.

CLASS 87s OLD AND NEW

Glancing at my *ABC* from 1989, I'd managed to underline all 36 Class 87s, along with all but four of Class 86. Although this seems like a considerable feat, especially as I'd only just started 'taking numbers' at this point, it has more to do with the ubiquity of these machines on the WCML and their high rates of availability.

Hornby was due to release an updated version of the old Lima product just as I finished this book, so the two models featured on pages 102–104 are of a true Italian vintage. Although, in their original condition, these models could look basic and betray their 1970s roots, they can still look reasonably good, especially once the worst of the moulded aberrations have been stripped away.

First to go are the diminutive buffers, along with the usual Lima moulded handrails. The nature of cab front detail will differ depending on the period being modelled and the two 87s featured represent the class at the beginning and end of their British-based careers. The same goes for the types of pantographs carried on the rooftops, along with other visible evidence of progress, such as external fire extinguishers and radio aerials.

Working on a second-hand Lima Class 87, the moulded jumper cables can be cut away without having to remove the junction boxes. Drill-out a pair of locating holes for the wire replacements, angling the tool to give the impression that the new cables are, indeed, sprouting from the boxes.

The new cables are then bent to shape (0.4mm wire) and fitted, along with new handrails.

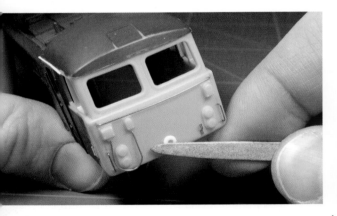

The moulded centre headlight is not so good on this model so, having removed it, a short length of ⅛in (3.2mm) diameter plastic rod was glued in place. Once set, the centre of the rod was marked and drilled-out to 0.060in (1.5mm) before a flat file reduced the remaining plastic to a height of 0.020in (0.5mm). This will represent the distinctive black rubber grommet fitted to the Class 87 when new. A small lamp bracket should also be fitted, folded up from Shawplan strips.

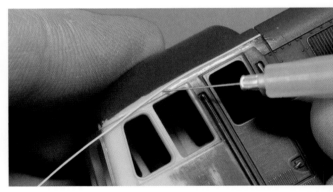

The rain strips over the cab doors can be better portrayed by fixing lengths of 0.010 × 0.020in (0.25 × 0.5mm) plastic strip, using a Deluxe Pin Flow tool, filled with Plastic Magic adhesive, to keep the job neat. As the glue sets, trim the strips to the desired length. The small sandbox filler hatches should be modified to suit the period in question as the hinges were originally along the vertical edge.

Turning to the chassis, new buffers, pipes, coupling and improvised electrical equipment connectors, from 0.070in (1.75mm) plastic rod and 0.010 × 0.100in (0.25 × 2.5mm) strip and conduit (0.7mm wire) may be added. The distinctive triangular footsteps are worth including; folded from 1mm wide strip brass, as are the guard irons attached to the front of the bogie frames. Sanding pipes, cut from fishing wire can be seen glued to the chassis and bogies, leaving sufficient slack to cope with curved track.

Various supplementary components were added, variously from the catalogues of Messrs Shawplan and A1, in addition to improvised parts formed of various sizes and forms of Evergreen plastic section and rod, plus some strip brass and nickel wire. Fishing wire even found employment as the distinctive sanding pipes that lead down from the chassis and attach to the front of each bogie. When fitting such items, be sure to leave enough slack to let the bogies rotate freely, but not an excessive amount so that the pipes drag along the rails! The wire is flexible and resilient enough to give long service, provided that the glue joints are secure.

One of those seemingly minor flourishes that brings about a big return is to drill-out the centre of the moulded marker lights, to a uniform depth of, say, 2mm and then to drop blobs of dark-red or light-grey paint into the recesses following application of the main livery. Once dry, another blob is then inserted, this time of a gloss varnish or Glue 'n' Glaze and this will mimic the effect of a glass lens. Be sure, though, to mark the exact centres of the lights carefully before drilling, lest the effect be ruined by wonky-looking lights!

The finished article looks far more impressive than the scruffy, second-hand model that I'd picked up at my local model shop for £25. Getting period-specific details right is important and we'll look more closely at this subject in Chapter 15.

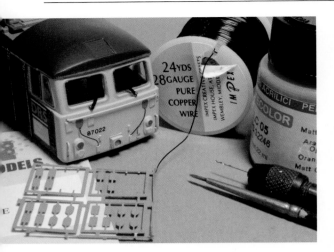

For this more recent representation of a Class 87, the different headlamp arrangement is clear, as are the plates over the former jumper cable boxes. The latter were cut from 0.010 × 0.060in (0.25 × 1.5mm) plastic strip, punched from behind to form bolt heads. New multiple working cables are in place using 0.3mm (30SWG) nickel jewellery wire along with retaining boxes of 0.040 × 0.020in (1.0 × 0.5mm) plastic. Small etched cable mountings, from A1, have been pre-painted in the regulation orange shade and fixed in place.

This DRS-liveried 87 portrays a short-lived experiment by the Carlisle-based operator in 2004. The later-period equipment included the red fire-extinguisher tanks and twin radio aerials on the locomotive's roof.

CLASS 91

I spend part of my regular journey to work scooting down the East Coast Main Line and have fancied a model of a GNER Class 91 for some time. Since this train-operating company's recent consignment to history, the need for a memento of this attractive livery was increased. So, taking a look at the Hornby model, what improvements can be made?

Firstly, the over-scale pantograph and rooftop details must be replaced, along with bufferbeam detail at both ends – including the missing valance at the 'slab' end – and removal of the tension lock coupling. Some etched windscreen wipers would help, while the wheels, for some reason, boast moulded spokes. As the illustrations (pages 105–108) show, once each facet was addressed, the finished model looks a far cry from the starting point, although, to Hornby's credit, the basis of the model is spot-on as far as the body shape and proportions are concerned.

Hornby's Class 91 model dates from 1988 and, other than the upgrade of the Ringfield-type motor to a five-pole version, remains unchanged since then. As a result, it has a tendency to look a little toy-like in terms of detail.

As I planned to upgrade the wheelsets, a few refinements to the bogie frames would add to the overall impression, so the over-sized footsteps were cut away.

Replacement footsteps were folded and soldered together from 1mm (0.040in) wide, 0.25mm (0.010in) thick brass strip, available from Mainly Trains. This was used both to form the basic square shape and then two strips of the same material were soldered to the upper faces to mimic the original pattern.

LEFT: New buffers and pipework (from A1 and Craftsman, respectively), plus etched chequer plate step boards and a cosmetic coupling hook and dropped buckeye, the latter a spare from a Heljan Class 33/1. Incidentally, the Craftsman jumper cables are supplied in the reverse pattern to what is required here (as shown loose in the foreground). Gentle bending and twisting of the white-metal component can correct this.

RIGHT: At the 'slab' end, the tension-lock coupling was removed from the bogie frame and a new valance assembled from 0.040in (1.0mm) plastic card, reinforced by ⅛in (3.2mm) Evergreen channel fitted along the bottom edge. A full complement of details were added to this end also as, this being intended as a static model, I hadn't to worry about a working coupling.

LEFT: Sanding pipes were added from fishing wire, just as on the Lima Class 87. As the wire is a little awkward to hold whilst the glue sets, apply a dab of Roket Blaster cyano accelerator to produce an instant bond, thus speeding up the job.

Perhaps the pièce de resistance of the modifications is the new pantograph, which is a fully working unit, permitting overhead power collection. This kit is produced by Hurst Models and portrays the Brecknell Willis High Speed pantograph. Manufactured as brass castings, the components are finely detailed, yet are tough enough to withstand everyday use. An ingenious springing system is incorporated, making use of a coil spring and a length of nylon thread. The kit comes with instructions that cover eight sheets of A4 paper and include full assembly illustrations, as well as wiring options. Although this is not an easy kit to build, taking the time to study and digest the instructions and proceeding in a methodical manner, it should not be beyond most modellers.

All three of the models seen in this chapter have received many hours' worth of attention to bring them up to scratch, particularly the more elderly 87s, but there is still more that could have been done. The moulded underframe equipment on the Lima models is good, but wouldn't it be nice to have perceptively individual components mounted underneath, just as in real life?

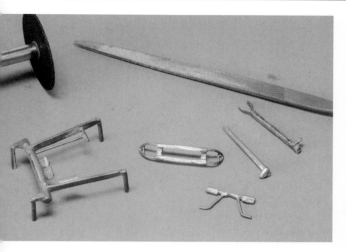

The Hurst Models' pantograph kit consists of a number of separate brass castings that require excess material cutting away. Use a carborundum cutting disc in a mini drill (wear goggles!) and finish off with a needle file.

The roof needs modifying to accept the new pantograph: the two holes furthest from the 'slab' end should be plugged with 0.080in (2.0mm) plastic rod and re-drilled a short distance along, using the pantograph base as a guide. The slide switch also needs removing and the hole blanking-off. Cut away the raised rim, glue some plastic sheet beneath and then fill the hole with modelling putty, sanding to a fine finish when set. Bypass the switch connection by fixing the two spade connectors directly to each other.

Follow the supplied instructions carefully and, a few hours later, you should have an impressive working pantograph. Prime and paint before final fitting to the locomotive.

With the new pantograph painted and fitted, an extra insulator was added (just visible beneath the lower arm) as described in the kit's instructions. This insulator is not supplied with the kit, instead being obtained from DC Kits.

ABOVE: A lightly weathered finish, particularly around the 'slab' end, and the extra details make for a much more convincing 91. The pattern of the new bogie footsteps can be appreciated.

BELOW: Etched windscreen wipers finish off the No.1 end. Further enhancements could include fitting of a working lighting unit and, maybe, opening out the horizontal 'fins' in the central side fairing, as is a feature of the real locomotives.

CHAPTER 10

Looking Underneath

Thankfully, as far as contemporary OO-gauge products are concerned, the days of monolithic representations of locomotive underframes have passed. Additionally, the wrong sort of equipment was sometimes rendered on the sides of the underframe 'block'. Some of the worst offenders emanated from Lima, namely the Class 47, 67 and 73. Such basic tooling has been thrown into stark relief by the beautiful underframes sported on recent models, with separately fitted components and exquisite renderings of compressors and other equipment.

When looking closely at real diesel and electric traction, it becomes clear that much more goes on 'downstairs' than it might at first seem. Filling and drain points, tank gauge dials, air-release valves, electrical conduit and pipe runs, make up the smaller details, while the bulk is usually formed of fuel and water tanks, battery compartments, compressors and air cylinders. Naturally, the amount of under-slung gear carried depends wholly on the locomotive's design. Some, such as the Class 40 and 47, had their fuel tanks mounted within the bodyshell, the lower containers holding water for the carriage heating boilers. Later modifications saw extra fuel tanks added or other forms of equipment fitted, such as air cylinders. It pays to check what should be hanging below your chosen prototype during the period in which it is portrayed.

There are quick underframe enhancements to undertake on most locomotives, consisting

Looking at the real thing tells us that underframe fittings and equipment differ between traction types and their various sub-divisions. Individual locomotives may also have their own eccentricities, showing evidence of repair and modification. This view of 45135 illustrates the long air cylinders and associated pipework and valves fitted to air brake-equipped 'Peaks'. Also visible is a range of filler and drain points, electrical conduit and safety catches to the battery compartment (picked out in yellow).

Bachmann do a good job of representing the cylinders on its range of air brake-equipped 'Peaks', with some lengths of piping also in place (right). The model on the left has had some extra runs of 0.45mm brass wire, drilled into the centre of the cylinders and linking into the main pipes. A regulating valve has also been fitted (top left), improvised from a steam locomotive injector castings.

of adding runs of brass wire (of various gauges), plus the odd bit of tubing and plastic section, to recreate filler and drain pipes, valves and conduit. Etched handwheels, seemingly more at home within a steam locomotive's cab, are perfect for many types of tank drain cocks, such as those fitted to the Class 08.

This view of Class 08, D3232, illustrates a few features missing from the Bachmann model, such as the fuel-filler point and pipe running across the locomotive, visible just beneath the bufferbeam. Also to be seen is the long coupling guard hanging behind the screw-link.

The fuel pipe is simple to form from 0.9mm (30SWG) wire, the end fillers being short lengths of 0.060in (1.5mm) plastic rod, drilled out to a shallow depth on one face to join with the wire. File the rod to a vaguely hexagonal shape to copy the profile of the filler cover. Small etched handwheels are available from Mainly Trains (ref.MT227) and are perfect for the drain cock, glued onto a short length of 0.3mm (30SWG) wire drilled into the chassis. The coupling guard is shaped from 0.010 × 0.100in (0.25 × 3.5mm) plastic strip.

Painted and weathered to blend in with the overall finish, the new parts look convincing, particularly the small handwheels, another of which has been fitted to the top edge of the bonnet.

At the other end of the 08, another coupling guard is in place along with a length of 1mm strip brass linking the footsteps and, behind that, a pipe links the twin tanks; made possible by dispensing with the tension lock couplings.

CREATING A HYBRID

The ubiquity of Lima's single Class 47 tooling was lamented in a previous chapter and the same comments extend to the chassis, which catered only for the non-boiler fitted machines. This limited the accuracy of the model to all but freight-sector allocations or later modified machines. Moreover, Lima insisted on producing a large, single block between the bogies, instead of a set of small boxes with a large clear gap in the middle. The bogie mouldings, on the other hand, are impressive for their time and, by replacing the central area, this 47 can look at home amongst more recent models.

The 'block' is simple enough to cut away, using a handsaw or circular cutting blade in a mini-drill. Don't use a knife here, as it presents too many risks to your fingers, the material being somewhat tough. Heljan, being a company that specializes in injection moulding, offer a lot of spare locomotive parts separately. These are supplied still attached to large sprues, just as if they'd come out of an Airfix kit. This approach is certainly to be applauded, as it can throw up all manner of useful bits and pieces including,

luckily enough, underframe components for the Class 47. I covered the use of these parts in an article for *Model Rail* a couple of years ago, fitting them to some Hornby 47s and this proved very popular. Therefore, I've briefly reprised the idea here, instead working on a Lima loco, plenty of which are still knocking around in people's collections. Heljan spares are, by the way, obtainable in Britain solely from Howes Models of Oxford.

Sometimes it pays to cut away the whole underframe area and start again! This Lima Class 47 chassis is being held firmly in a vice while a circular saw bit is used in a mini drill to cut through the moulding. Leave a few millimetres of waste to prevent any mishaps, and finish the job with a broad flat file.

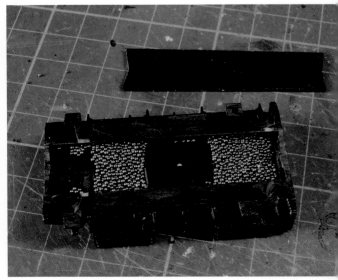

The resulting hole ought to be filled in with a slab of thick (0.080in/2.0mm) plastic card, reinforced with plastic angle. Let this set completely before going any further.

Use epoxy glue to secure the new tanks to the underside of the chassis, clamping and leaving aside to set entirely. After this, some extra weight will still be helpful and I used epoxy again to stick some scrap Hornby weights on to the bed of the underframe.

Heljan Class 47 underframe components have been available as spare parts recently, a large sprue containing a choice of three different tank and battery box variations to suit particular prototypes. Assemble the appropriate set, gluing the outer mouldings to the central piece and filling the voids with lead shot. Seal this inside by cutting some plastic card to fit into the recess. Ensure a tight fit and a strong joint, adding some filler if necessary.

The replacement tanks and battery boxes make a massive visual difference to this Lima 47, doing justice to the attractive bogie mouldings.

SCRATCHBUILDING COMPONENTS

As expected, Hornby wasted little time in tweaking and repackaging the cream of the former Lima products that it had acquired. One of the first re-releases was the handsome Class 67 that featured one of Lima's higher specification power units. The chief area for improvement is the central portion of the underframe, consisting of a one-piece moulding incorporating the fuel tank, battery compartment and a rather shoddy rendition of a set of air cylinders. As this portion is self-contained and is easily demountable (two screws hold it in place), I wonder if Hornby will commission a tooling for a replacement unit?

Once the steel weights have been taken out, the unit can be cut into its constituent parts. The air cylinders are best consigned to the waste bin, while the tank and battery box will need the open ends filling with thick plastic card and the corners reinforced with plastic angle. The steel weights could be cut to fit inside the new

The ex-Lima Class 67, now in the Hornby catalogue, is a splendid model in a lot of ways but is let down by the one-piece slab underframe. However, it is easy to detach and chop into separate components. Here, the fuel tank and battery box have been separated and the open faces filled-in with plastic card. It's wise to reinforce the corners with plastic angle if filling with lead shot as the units will become quite heavy. Create a pair of lids and fit them tightly in place and set aside for the glue to harden.

The exposed end of the battery box has a rippled face, something that is clearly visible on the real locomotives, recreated on my model by laminating the box with slatted embossed plastic card, framed with 0.020 × 0.060in (0.5 × 2.0mm) strip.

compartments or lead shot poured in and the tops sealed with more plastic card. As the lead will render the boxes quite heavy, the glue joints will have to be very strong, so, therefore, ensure the sides and lids are a good fit and strengthen with extra plastic where possible. Be aware that a pair of mounting bolts protrude a few millimetres below the chassis and the lid of the fuel tank must be recessed slightly to accommodate this.

The twin air tanks are better represented by scratchbuilding some individual cylinders using lengths of ¼in (6.3mm) plastic tube, the open ends having been filled with suitable modelling putty and shaped to a rounded profile by mounting the piece in the chuck of a drill and turned on a slow speed against a file and abrasive paper. Regulator valves can also be produced in this way, using various patterns of needle files to create a realistic profile; the knife-edge of a triangular section file is perfect for inserting sharp lines around the rod and tube.

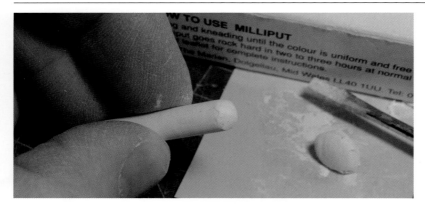

To better represent the twin air cylinders, lengths of ¼in (6.4mm) plastic tube can be cut to size and the ends filled with Milliput modelling putty.

Mount a mini drill in a vice and load the plastic tubes. The ends can be dressed by turning them against a file and polishing against fine abrasive paper. Other components can also be shaped in this way, such as this valve being profiled against a round file.

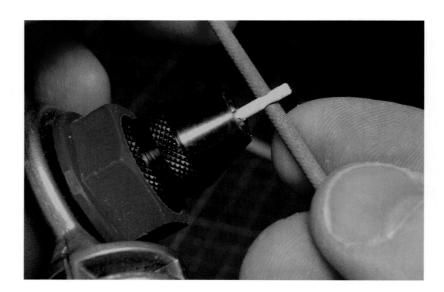

The air tanks are mounted on to plastic girders, shimmed to the right height with scraps of plastic card. Photographs should be studied to recreate the various pipe runs and valve fittings.

Another detail worthy of inclusion is the AWS equipment, fitted to the end of the fuel tank. Make sure there's room for the bogie to rotate.

Separately defined components look much more convincing.

A HALFWAY HOUSE

If you don't fancy jumping into scratchbuilding new components, a slightly easier route to greater detail is to make the most of what is already fitted to the model. A good starting point for this is the Hornby (ex-Lima) Class 73, purely because of how the chassis is assembled. Consisting of Lima's usual solid central block, clip-on sides contain shallow, moulded representations of the fuel tanks, compressors, generator and other equipment. After prising these off, the block can be cut away, leaving just the bulk of the fuel tank behind.

As with the 47 project, the floor pan and fuel tank's sides should be filled in with plastic card and lead shot poured into the tank's void, before it is sealed up. It's then possible to extract various separate components from the side overlays, trimming away waste material

The Hornby Class 73 is another former Lima product that is betrayed by the boxy nature of the underframe. Luckily, the moulded relief panels simply unclip from the chassis sides and can then be cut into individual components, beefed-up with plastic rod and section, then re-fitted to the modified underframe. The fuel tanks are the only area left as one piece, the ends having been blanked-in and the void filled with lead shot.

and refitting to the chassis floor, propped up on scraps of plastic or suspended from pieces of angle. To create more of a sense of depth, back-up the larger parts, such as the generator and compressor, with plastic strip and tube, using filler and files to blend in any joints. Linking the equipment with runs of wire and tubing will complete a convincing picture. Just remember to leave enough clearance for the bogies to turn freely.

It seems like a common-sense approach to devote an equal amount of energy to the enhancement of a locomotive's underframe as is spent on the bodyshell and, if utilizing r-t-r products that are a little longer in the tooth, some degree of chassis work comes with the territory.

This Class 73 has received a good amount of detailing work: moulded grilles replaced; new bufferbeam detail; bogie footsteps; enhanced underframe components; wire handrails. So much work, in fact, that a new paint job was necessary and this rather fetching Merseyrail-branded scheme was chosen.

ABOVE: As well as adding extra components, such as the various lengths of piping, drain points and switch handle seen here, this Lima HST power car has also had the slab-sided moulding trimmed here and there to give a feeling of the components being individually mounted, particularly the compressor assembly (left).

BELOW: At the time of writing, Heljan had yet to offer its Class 26 model with the later air-brake modification. On the real things, the steam-heat boilers were isolated and the under-slung water tanks replaced by steel cradles containing a pair of air cylinders and other associated valves and pipes. This model has had such an arrangement scratchbuilt from plastic section and rod, surmising most of the dimensions from careful study of photographs. The small straps around the air tanks were formed from thin strips of electrical insulation tape and the relief valve is just two pieces of different diameter rod stuck together; all simple methods that combine to produce a very professional finish.

CHAPTER 11

Painting

Painting is an essential part of all branches of model-making, regardless of the level of work being carried out; even adding the factory-supplied detailing parts to a loco involves some addition of colour. Applying new components or undertaking modification work will, naturally, lead to a greater degree of repainting, from a little touching-in, to applying an entirely new livery.

An understanding of the various types of paint, varnish and application methods will always be helpful. Entire books have been written on this subject (or small elements of it) and a comprehensive guide is not possible in a single chapter. However, treat the following as an overview of techniques and consider some of the recommendations made following my own trials and tribulations.

PREPARATION

As with so much in life, preparation is the key to success and a few shortcuts here and there will often tell in the final result. A factory-finish will have to be rubbed-down in order to give the new paint a 'key' to stick properly and any printed logos or numbers flattened, otherwise they will show through later. Various grades of wet-or-dry abrasive paper, cut into small strips, are ideal for this purpose, with plenty of clean water to keep the paper from clogging and to produce an even surface. Progressing to a super-fine grade (1,000 or 1,500) should see any scratches removed from the coarser grades. I prefer to finish with 0000grade wire wool as this reaches into recesses and around corners easily but, as with the abra-

sive papers, extreme care must be taken not to damage any delicate details or moulded profiles. Indeed, if a full or partial repaint is envisaged from the offing, then such surfaces should be prepared in this way before new etched components or wire handrails are fitted.

Unless painting bituminous underseal on to a car's underframe, all types of paint require a clean, grease-free surface on which to adhere. We're not only talking about lubricating oil or grease here, but also residues from fingers and hands. In my time working for Merseyside Museums, I was constantly reminded of the need to wear cotton gloves when handling fine furniture or precious artefacts, as particles of sweat and the natural oils present on everyone's hands can have a detrimental effect on many materials over time. I've never felt conscious of having particularly sweaty palms, but following such training in conservation, it's hard not to develop a compulsive hand-washing disorder!

Anyway, after handling a model that is to be painted, give it a good clean with either a dash of white spirit on a scrap of lint-free cloth or, if the whole bodyshell is to be treated, an overall wash with detergent and clean water will do the trick. Never use anything such as a washing-up liquid, as these contain residue that leaves dishes gleaming but anything else impermeable to paint. A cream cleanser, or 'Cif'-branded cleaner is best here, rubbing the surface with an old (but clean) toothbrush to remove any gunk, dust or filings. If brass components have been soldered, then be sure to take a zealous approach to removing all traces of flux in the same way. Allow the model to dry naturally, perhaps in a warm corner somewhere overnight, lain on a bed of kitchen tissue. Any further handling, such as applying masking, should be done with as little physical contact as possible, perhaps wearing gloves to prevent further contamination.

Fresh paintwork contaminated by dust particles is an annoying thing to have to repair. Undercoats are not such a big deal as the surface can be redressed with wet/dry or wire wool and a light coat reapplied. However, fibres stuck in a top colour or varnish coat is about as frustrating as it gets. Having recently been adopted by a cat, I've been finding white hairs everywhere and, even though I may be careful about keeping my painting 'zone' clean, it doesn't help when you enter it wearing a jumper that sheds fibres or animal hair whilst working.

Choosing a good primer is as important as the quality of the paints used for the topcoats as, without a sound footing, any subsequent applications will not be up to scratch. Even the touching-in of small parts can benefit from the use of a priming coat, especially where etched or cast metal components are concerned, and a thin covering of matt white or grey enamel, applied by brush, is sufficient. For treating large areas, aerosol car primers are very useful, if applied with caution. Model paint manufacturers offer dedicated pots of primer and, when applied with an airbrush, can produce better results than aerosols, as these tend to emit a heavy and dense coat that is not always easy to control.

Compatibility of different paints is an important point to consider, as mixing some types can have negative repercussions. For instance, spraying a car aerosol primer on to a factory-painted model will usually be safe. However, spray the same paint on to any enamel paint and the latter will instantly start to peel and leave a terrible mess. Conversely, applying enamels on top of the same primer will be fine! When in doubt, always test on a scrap piece of rolling stock.

MASKING

Patch-painting to cover new components can involve priming and painting anything from a small area of a roof, to a whole cab front. Sometimes, features of the bodywork can work in your favour, presenting a natural 'line' against which to join old and new paint; cab doors, grilles and roof lines are all helpful. Much detailing work concentrates on cab fronts and this new equipment can be treated by a new application of a front warning panel.

Whenever working with bare materials, be they new components or exposed plastic, a suitable undercoat should always be employed. A good aerosol-based primer is perfect for larger areas, while smaller parts should be treated by hand or airbrush. Railway liveries are also supplied in aerosols but the quality of finish from this medium is inferior to applying by airbrush.

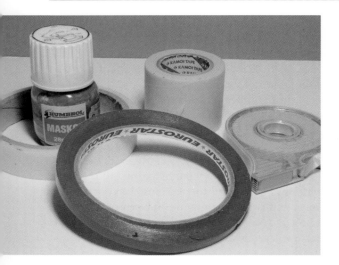

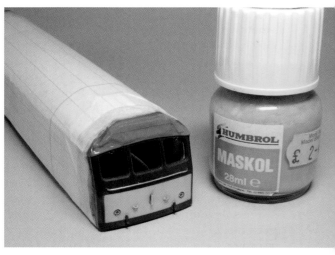

Keeping a stock of good-quality masking tapes is recommended. Different sizes are useful and a vinyl-based tape, such as the red Eurostar reel seen here, has its own benefits. A liquid masking fluid is also essential for sealing tape joints or for covering awkward or uneven areas.

Sometimes, you can get away with repainting only a small area. Hopefully, a natural division can be utilized, such as bodywork panels or, as in this case, by repainting the cab ends only. Luckily, it was intended to replace the small warning panel with full yellow ends for this early 1970s-era Class 25. Mask the model carefully, using a vinyl tape to cope with curves and minor undulations, as its flexibility will help. Using scrap paper to cover large areas is an economy measure. Seal any gaps or tape joints with Maskol.

Whatever extent of repainting is to be done, a high-quality masking tape is fundamental to achieving satisfying results. It pays to keep a variety of sizes and types at hand to suit different jobs and to economize, e.g. using wider tapes for larger surfaces. Vinyl-type reels, such as those produced by Electrostar, are excellent at coping with undulating surfaces and for working into tight corners. The 'stretchy' properties also help it run around curved profiles accurately and reliably. Another thrift tip is to use one of these vinyl tapes for masking up to the paint's 'joint' line, then backing this up with wider, cheaper tape (such as that made by Tamiya) that is excellent in its own way but without the ability to produce a knife-edge paint line.

Some general decorator's tapes are suitable for what I'd call 'non-essential' jobs, such as securing expanses of scrap paper over large areas, but allowing them into contact with previously painted surfaces may end in trouble. Regardless of tape, ensure that any previous coats

have hardened completely before applying more masking.

An alternative to tape is clear masking film. I've only discovered the benefits of this relatively recently, despite having been aware of it since my art school days; it just took ten years for the old bean to creak into gear and realize the potential in model-making! I use Ultra Mask film, from The Airbrush Company, which is available in A4-sized sheets or in long rolls for those of us that get through it rather quickly. This translucent film can be easily cut to a beautifully sharp edge, provided, of course, that a fresh blade is used. For the more complex patterns, a fine point blade will help cut any tight curves or swirls. This masking method lends itself to reproducing modern post-privatization schemes that are often plastered across the sides of locomotives, multiple units and rolling stock. However, it's also unsurpassable for the accurate masking of early BR warning panels. To make cutting of the film more accurate, a Robo plotter/cutter machine is offered from the same company and this allows super-accurate masks to be drawn on a computer and then the film is scored by laser, leaving it only to be peeled from the backing. This is not a cheap piece of kit but it does open up possibilities for producing some professional-quality models regardless of the complexity of the graphic work. If you're a whizz on a PC, capturing a logotype as a digital image, then transferring it to the cutter via a suitable manipulation software cuts out a lot of work.

The film has a certain amount of flexibility built into the material but for protruding features such as headlights or brackets, just a slit with a knife will allow the offending item to peep through and some scraps of film can be stuck over as a patch. Any such patches or joints in tape or film should always be covered with a liquid masking fluid to secure against any ingress of paint. Humbrol Maskol is freely available in model shops and this pinkish liquid sets to a rubbery film after a few minutes and is impermeable to oil- or water-based paints. Maskol can also be utilized to cope with awkward areas, where a tape or film can't be manipulated into, or for covering glazing and light lenses when applying a varnish coat.

Masking can vary in difficulty but, whenever raised details are encountered, it's essential to avoid any gaps where the topcoats will seep through. A clear masking film, such as Ultra Mask, is perfect for coping with odd shapes and uneven surfaces: simply cut a small recess for any protrusions to fit through and then add a healthy blob of Maskol to seal.

With careful masking and thoughtful ordering of colour applications, more complex liveries can be applied. Thin stripes, such as the waist-high lining on some BR green machines, can best be applied with transfers such as seen here, using decals from the Fox range.

PAINT AND VARNISH

Enamel paints are well-established in the psyche of most modellers, certainly of those of us who grew up using tinlets of Humbrol or Revell colours on our Airfix kits. This type of oil-based paint offers plenty of benefits in terms of workability and quality of finish, but results do depend on the method and quality of application. The Humbrol colour range is quite extensive in terms of primary and general colours, as well as specific military shades. As for railway-based subjects, Humbrol at one time offered a limited choice of colours for this market but were discontinued some time ago. A mixing pack is still available, however, with a booklet of swatches and guides for mixing specific liveries. Now that the Humbrol brand has been acquired by Hornby, there has recently been a re-launch of the railway range.

Most of the Humbrol paints produce acceptable results, and their cheapness and wide availability play in their favour. But, in my opinion, the quality of pigment can be inconsistent, while some colours tend to dry too quickly, making application difficult (unless airbrushing). The No.33 'matt black' is particularly feisty in this respect, the paint sometimes forming a skin while the tin is open, although it does give a splendid ultra-flat finish.

Phoenix Precision Paints boast a broad range of railway colours, stretching from the 'modern' era back to pre-Grouping companies. The 'dull' formulas dry to a very matt sheen and require at least a couple of coats of gloss varnish before any decals will adhere to the surface. Alternatively, the Railmatch brand of coaching enamels is marketed by Howes Models and this range has grown markedly over the last ten years or so. Uniquely supplied in glass jars, rather than tins,

There are plenty of model paints on the market, in oil-based enamel or water-based acrylic formulations, each supported by appropriate thinning mediums. For railway colours, Railmatch and Phoenix Precision have established themselves as household names, while Humbrol and Lifecolor boast extensive ranges of useful shades.

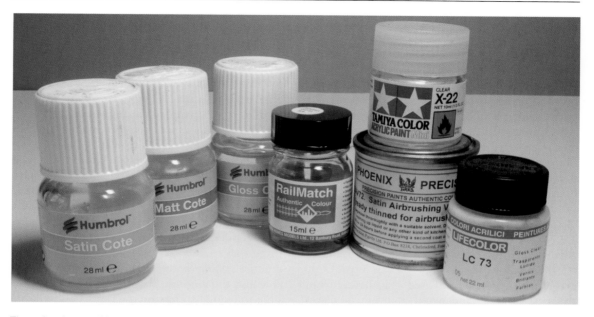

There is also a wide choice of enamel or acrylic varnishes, each with their own advantages. An overall coating of a satin or matt varnish acts to seal any decals but will also give the model a more even finish, especially when blending in new paintwork.

the paints are formulated to a thinner viscosity than other brands, making it almost ready for use in an airbrush but awkward to apply by hand. Another, slightly less well-known brand of railway colours is Cherry Model paints and these are available via Fox Transfers.

Another form of solvent-based paint is the cellulose formula, as can be found in tins of automotive paint in stores such as Halfords. Use of this paint requires caution and can be destructive to certain plastics if not used correctly. Rapid-drying, so reducing the risk of dust settling, it means that spraying is really the only suitable application method. It can, however, provide a very hardwearing and superior finish. Another advantage is that, if used to apply livery and varnish coats, it will not be upset by subsequently using enamels for a weathering job, regardless of how much enamel thinner is daubed on to it. No proprietary range of model paints are offered in cellulose, so it must be a case of having it mixed for you. This is not too difficult, as most auto-

motive paint suppliers will be happy to help as long as a sample is provided to match to a colour chart.

Water-based acrylic paints have only lately gained popularity among railway modellers, despite having already been used in other disciplines for a while. Some modellers still frown at the thought of using water-based paint for applying liveries and, I'm afraid, I'm yet to be satisfied with the results of each formula that I've tried. Enamel and cellulose paint offer more even and 'deep' finishes, with more lustre and hardness, whilst acrylics tend to look a little 'flat' in comparison. The rapid drying of acrylics, as with cellulose, can either be a blessing or a curse and, once dry, they are very difficult to remove. Acrylics are, on the other hand, perfectly acceptable for touching-in new details.

As a sealing coat of varnish is likely to be the final covering on a model, it's naturally important to choose a good-quality formula. When using certain brands of decals, a water-based varnish may have to be used, but some brands can have problems in sticking to the gloss surface, as prepared for the application of transfers, especially if an enamel gloss has been used. Acrylic varnishes do not tend to be as hardwearing as oil-based finishes; an important factor, if any weathering or distressing is to be employed. Humbrol offers tins of matt, satin and gloss varnish, as well as jars of a faster-drying formula, known as Satincote, Mattcote and Glosscote, although these are not as durable as the clear coats in the Phoenix and Railmatch ranges.

APPLICATION

Before applying any paints, it's important to consider some basic safety precautions. Only ever work in a well-ventilated space, away from any pets or kids, and avoid painting in damp or cold conditions, and definitely not anywhere near a gas or electric heater. Always wear a mask if spraying paint, regardless of working into an extraction booth or not. Use a proper mask that fits properly and that meets the appropriate European standards for paint-vapour particles; you wouldn't wear a woolly hat to go motorcycle racing, would you? Being bearded, I have a few problems with ensuring a good seal around

my face mask and usually resort to wrapping an old, moistened handkerchief inside to seal the edges. It's frighteningly easy not to realize what you're breathing-in at the time but, come to blow your nose later and out pours some BR blue excreta. Considering that many railway-specific model paints contain lead chromate on top of the other noxious solvents, this is not good for you.

Good-quality paintbrushes should be used wherever possible, as they are more likely to keep their shape and not to shed bristles while working. Aerosols have their uses, especially where primer coats are concerned. Livery colours can be sprayed from these cans but it's not something that I freely recommend as being of 'good practice'. Spray patterns can be very unpredictable and the amount of paint emitted is impossible to regulate, creating the risk of obliterating fine detail with an excessively thick coating.

If you only intend to undertake projects requiring the odd small part to be decorated, or the addition of light weathering, then the costs involved in acquiring an airbrush may be avoided. However, for application of new liveries and full repaints, plus more involved weathering tasks, a good-quality airbrush is a necessary luxury. The initial outlay will repay itself soon

As well as an airbrush, a reliable source of compressed air is required, as well as a safe place in which to work. Small compressors with storage tanks are now much less costly than in the past and some form of fume extraction is a must. Working in a shed like this provides plenty of natural light and ventilation, although the room should be kept as dust-free as possible.

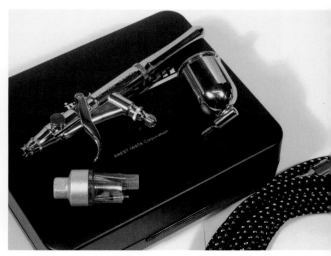

For many small jobs, such as touching-in new detailing components, a fine brush will suffice to apply the paint. For this Bachmann Class 37, the lamp brackets were undercoated with a shade of green Humbrol acrylic before a topcoat of Railmatch BR green. The yellow panel was also corrected in this way; the tail light recesses being all-green rather than yellow as supplied out-of-the-box.

Investment in a good quality airbrush will be rewarded with superior results and less frustration. It seems counter-productive to expend much time and effort on a model, to then compromise with a sub-standard finish. This Iwata TR2 airbrush set is competitively priced and versatile enough to be used for all painting and weathering jobs.

enough, particularly if numerous locomotive, carriage and wagon projects are in the pipeline. A cheap airbrush, that is one that retails for less than £50, will invariably prove to be a waste of time and money, as the results they offer are simply not worth it. Airbrushing is another specific modelling skill that is good to master, and struggling with a poor instrument will only serve to frustrate and to destroy any sense of enjoyment. A choice of single, dual-acting and gravity or suction-feed airbrushes are obtainable; each

with their own benefits and pitfalls. It's too big a subject for discussion here but I will recommend that a respected brand is chosen, such as Iwata or Badger, and the type of tool chosen to suit the projected uses. Make an informed purchase by doing a little research from books and magazine articles, and there are plenty of instructional DVDs out there from which to form an idea of what's involved. Moreover, practical demonstration classes are offered, such as those run by The Airbrush Company.

The most onerous part of painting is the clearing up and this is especially important when airbrushing in order to maintain performance of your equipment. Aerosol cleaners are very handy in this respect as a few squirts will flush out any remaining paint, leaving the tool ready for the next colour. A thorough dismantling and cleaning is, however, recommended after each session.

If spraying with an airbrush, the hardest trick to master is the correct thinning of paints. Whether using enamels or acrylics, I employ the 'drip test' to check the viscosity. Add the paint to a mixing jar then add a couple of drops of thinner using a bulb pipette. After stirring for a few moments, lift out the spatula and see if the mixture falls off the tool in self-contained drops. If it does, then it's ready, but if the drops are elongated then add more thinners, a few drops at a time, and repeat the process.

Good-quality compressors are much cheaper these days than when I began as a model-maker, especially those units fitted with an air cylinder. Without, the air can 'pulse' out of the airbrush in harmony with the pump's piston, creating an uneven finish and putting strain on the motor if used for long periods at a stretch. Having a store of air means the motor only kicks in to keep the pressure topped-up. A pressure gauge is also useful, as certain paints and application methods require lower or higher pressures. In-line water traps are also essential as, wherever you may be working, condensing air forms water droplets and these can enter the airbrush and appear as big blobs on your model. Realistically, a budget of around £200 should be allotted for an airbrush and compressor and, though that might sound like a lot of money, it roughly equates to the cost of two of today's 'high spec' locomotives. Cans of aerosol-based airbrush propellant are a poor substitute, tending as they do to freeze after a minute of use and lasting for only a short time.

Attempting to blend-in new paintwork can be difficult, as the shades employed by r-t-r manufacturers and paint suppliers often vary. This Heljan Class 27 has received a new radiator grille and, after careful masking and undercoating, a thin coat of BR blue is being sprayed over the local area.

In an attempt to 'soften' the edges of the new paint, the masking was moved to cover sensitive areas, such as the yellow ends, glazing and the grey roof panel. The same BR blue was then misted over a slightly broader area.

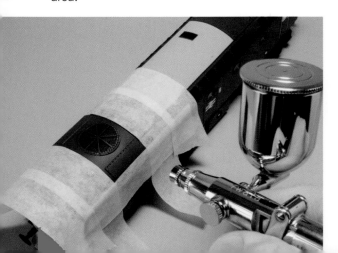

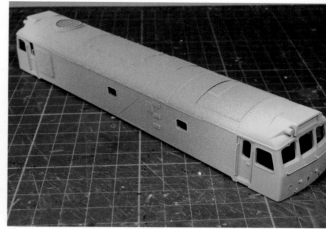

The joys of weathering! A light spray of exhaust smoke conceals any minor discrepancies.

If a full repaint is necessary, prepare the model by cleaning and drying thoroughly before spraying a coat of grey primer. Lighter colours are best applied first and, in this case, a light coat of matt white preceded the warning yellow ends. Allow each coat to harden completely, at least overnight, before masking and applying further coats.

If any stray paint does get through the masking, use a cocktail stick dipped in some white spirit or T-Cut to soften the excess and rub it away with a cotton bud.

ABOVE: Thin stripes, such as cantrail warning lines, are also available in transfers form, but I find that using a bow pen is much quicker. Load the pen with a brush-full of paint, thinned if necessary (Most Lifecolor acrylics come supplied in the perfect viscosity) and wipe the outside of the jaws clean.

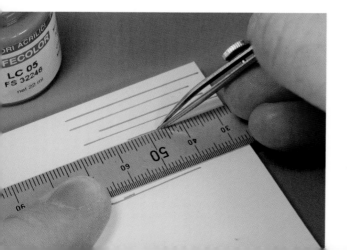

LEFT: Use the thumbwheel to adjust the thickness of line, practising on scrap paper until happy.

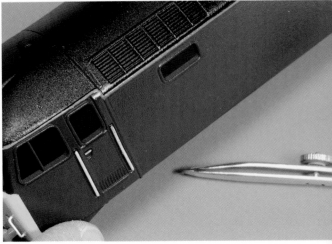

Draw the bow pen across the model's surface, against a straight edge, using only light pressure. If the paint clogs, rinse the pen and start again. Be prepared to clean and refill the pen for every individual application and protect the paintwork beneath the ruler with paper.

Accurate use of the bow pen is a useful skill to master, as it speeds up the application of a typical warning stripe by a ratio of at least 10:1. Any small gaps that are not easy to do with the pen should be touched-in with a 00000 brush.

STRIPPING

'What if it all goes wrong?', I hear you ask. As I've mentioned, acrylics can be hard to remove and careful abrading with wet/dry paper is necessary before over-painting; this is far from ideal. Oil- and solvent-based paints, on the other hand, can be stripped by applying suitable chemicals, thus preserving any delicate moulded detail from abrasives. Depending on the formula, the factory-applied finish may or may not be removed. However, be warned that most stripping compounds will destroy superglue joints, so take care not to lose any lamp brackets or grilles that will

come adrift. Follow the instructions for application and removal and be sure to wear rubber gloves and a pair of eye goggles to guard against splashes. Only ever use a stripping compound that is designed for use on plastic models as DIY strippers, such as Nitromors, will melt your locomotive instantly.

Detail cannot stand alone on a model. The degree of realism imparted, regardless of how many fine and intricate components are added, will always be dependant upon the quality of finish. Therefore, adequate preparation and an accomplished painting and varnishing technique are essential.

As with most skills, practise is the only way of acquiring the experience and confidence. Don't worry if you make mistakes . . . there's always paint stripper! Use only a dedicated model paint stripper on plastic models to avoid a major disaster. Modelstrip is available from good model shops and comes in a thick paste. Other types are available, such as a liquid formula from Phoenix Precision.

CHAPTER 12

Weathering

Railways, be they steam, diesel or electric-powered, are inherently dirty environments. Not only are they almost exclusively outdoors, but they run in all weathers, at high speeds, through industrial, urban or rural environments. The principle of running steel wheels on steel rails creates millions of tiny particles of metal, especially when friction brakes are applied, and this dust is spread all over the place. Fuel, heavy lubricating oil, thick grease and liquid coolants are utilized in enormous quantities and, invariably, leakage occurs.

Discharging toilets spray all sorts of unpleasantness around underframes, exhaust fumes containing burnt oil, carbon and other noxious chemicals stain the paintwork of engines and stock. Freight loads such as coal, iron ore, cement and limestone emit dust that clings to a locomotive and then, when it rains, becomes a thick sludge running in streaks down the bodywork. Damaged and chipped paint begins to blister as water ingress allows the steelwork to rust.

No matter how studiously a railway company cleans its trains at the end of every day's service, due to the presence of overhead wires or access issues, locomotive roofs are rarely cleaned, nor are underframes unless general repairs are carried out. Taking one look at any train, no matter how well maintained, will reveal some degree of muck trapped into recesses or behind grilles. Dirty hand marks around the cab doors, exhaust staining, even dead birds and insects on the cab fronts. Moreover, cleaning can actually create some interesting weathering patterns, such as faded paintwork (from excessive cleaning) or streaking where concentrated roof dirt has been disturbed and is running down the sides. Greased buffer-heads and working surfaces invariably catch all sorts of filth.

This decrepit-looking Class 31, 31556, may be an extreme example but many locomotives spend most of their careers accumulating dirt and grime, as they operate in all conditions and are rarely stored indoors. It all depends how often and how well they're cleaned. Take a look at the complexity of shades on the underframes and the vertical streaking of the bodywork.

WHY WEATHER?

With all this in mind, it may now seem pointless to ask the question: 'why weather a model locomotive?'. A number of specific reasons are thus:

- Creating a heightened level of realism.
- Using the technique to disguise any modification work and the resulting new paintwork.
- To help blend a model into its miniature surroundings.
- Providing an opportunity for customization.

Factory-produced models are designed to be uniformly finished and so live up to an expected level of quality control. This is excellent news for the consumer in terms of value for money but, no matter how well-finished a model may be, it will still only appear as a model. However, in order for it to look at home in the surroundings of a detailed miniature environment, some degree of weathering is required.

The importance of research has already been stated and it is equally important as a basis for a convincing weathering job. Studying the real thing will reveal a myriad of shades within what might initially be dismissed as a dirty brown underframe or fuel tank. Look at which areas of the bodywork suffer the most wear and tear, such as around door handles, kick steps below doors and buffer heads. Don't forget, also, that paintwork exposed to the elements for years can fade in uneven patches and streaks so, unless representing a prototype fresh from the paint shop, an immaculate and even coating may not be appropriate.

The practice of weathering and distressing has long been popular with military modellers and many products aimed primarily at this market have cross-over appeal to railway modellers, such as sets of acrylic paint, weathering powders and pigments. Railway paint brands are catching on, however, with specific weathering shades becoming popular in enamel and acrylic formulas.

There are many ways in which you can go about weathering and these images (pages 131–137) will, hopefully, provide an idea of the materials and techniques involved. Again, it's another technique that must be honed and fine-tuned through trial and error, and plenty of practise. Indeed, it's a good way to give derelict or unwanted rolling stock a reprieve from the scrap heap for use as practise pieces. A number of books have been written on the subject but none has surpassed *The Art of Weathering* by Martyn Welch (Wild Swan 1993; ISBN 978 1 874103 11 0) for its sheer depth of coverage and engaging text. A good many instructional DVDs on this subject are also on the market (including one made by yours truly!) and being able to see the techniques in action, rather than reading about them, helps enormously. Previously, I've mentioned practical workshops run by The Airbrush Company – courses in weathering are also offered. Don't be put off by books, magazines or films offering demonstrations in other modelling disciplines, as these can be just as informative; the same basic principles apply.

A lightly weathered finish can be achieved with minimal materials and equipment, careful application creating a more sensitive finish than most factory-applied weathering. Even ex-works diesels will have some exhaust staining on the roof panels and this can be brushed around the outlet ports using a 'smoke' shade of weathering powder or from a pack of Tamiya Weathering Master pigments. Use a soft paintbrush to apply powders, but never blow away the excess with your breath as you'll invariably end up with a trail of spittle across the model – unpleasant but true. Ensure that the staining reaches into any panel lines and recesses by dabbing the brush or applicator into the surface and any streaking should follow a vertical course as if rain has washed the muck downwards.

The Tamiya pigments can also be utilized to portray track dirt and brake dust across underframe areas and lower body surfaces. The supplied sponge applicator can be supplemented with cotton buds and a toothbrush to reach awkward spots. With all weathering techniques, experiment on an old wagon or carriage to gain a feel for the material before starting on an expensive model. At least with the Tamiya pigments, any mistakes can be cleaned up with a little white spirit.

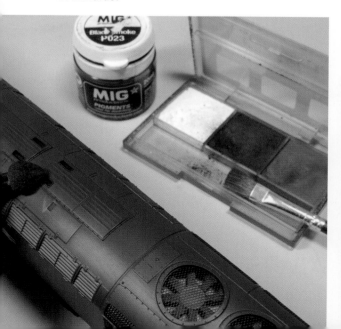

Just a hint of dirt and dust on this new Hornby Class 56 gives it a convincing 'lived-in' feel of a machine that has only been in service for a short while. The wealth of bogie and underframe detail is actually enhanced after this attention, as are the side grilles that have been rubbed with 'gunmetal' from the Tamiya pack. A mix of matt black, brown and dark grey acrylics stippled on to the buffer heads mimic the thick grease applied to these surfaces in real life.

The subtle use of weathering powders and pigments on the roof, around the exhaust ports, gives an impression of drifting fumes and oily deposits. Brushing away excess with a toothbrush leaves most of the 'muck' in between the panels.

For a greater degree of weathering, using a good airbrush is probably the best application method and treating the chassis and body separately simplifies the job. Here, Railmatch 'Track Dirt' enamel has been sprayed on to the underframe before supplementing with various lighter and darker shades to add a little variation in tone to certain areas. Mixing in a little Railmatch 'Dark Rust' creates a look of brake dust, while some 'Roof Dirt' will add darker streaks – ideal around fuel tanks and oil draining points.

LEFT: Working on a bodyshell, the roof is the best place to start. For an overall covering of grime, spray into any recesses first, working from each angle. This Class 67 silencer arrangement proves a little awkward to work the paint into, and a patch of bright red paint amongst the smoke staining will spoil the effect. I like to add a few drops of Humbrol Metalcote 'gunmetal' (No.27004) to a mix of Railmatch 'Roof Dirt' enamel as this leaves an oily-looking residue that is most realistic.

ABOVE: The rest of the roof can then be sprayed as desired, lightening the covering away from the exhaust port. It's often wise to mask-up the windows whilst weathering.

ABOVE: Masking the glazing is important, either covering the entire window or just where the wiper blades have worked. Maskol fluid has been used here, but tape or film can be cut to shape and fixed in place just as easily. A misting of track dirt and brake dust, up from the lower edges, mimics reality and the ends often take a battering from the elements or, in high summer, from dead insects.

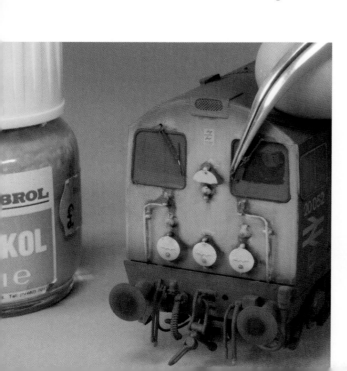

LEFT: Once the paint has dried, the window masking can be removed to reveal the wiper patterns. Mostly, drivers and shed staff kept windscreens fairly clean, regardless of the state of the rest of the locomotive, but only when the machine was being stabled or serviced, allowing plenty of time for such muck to accumulate out 'on the road', especially when working under hopper chutes at collieries, for example. This Class 20 has purposely mismatched blobs of yellow paint covering new or modified components, mirroring a photograph of a sister machine that had some rust patches treated in a similar manner; very convenient for the modeller!

Instead of using ready-mixed weathering paints, I often assemble my own shades for certain projects. My palette nearly always consists of just three Humbrol enamel colours: No.27004 Metal Cote 'gunmetal'; No.29 'brown'; No.62 'leather'. Sometimes, I'll use No.113 'rust' and 112 'tarmac' and just about every shade of 'dirt' is achievable with this small selection.

As either an alternative or an addition to airbrushing weathering colours, apply a mix of enamel 'dirt' by hand. Working in small areas at a time, brush on the mix and ensure that it sits into all nooks and crannies . . .

. . . then immediately rub the paint away with a dry cotton bud, working always in vertical strokes. Change the bud regularly and work until most or all of the paint has been removed, although leaving it inside any recesses. This leaves a streaky sort of appearance to the paintwork and, by buffing with a toothbrush, the metallic particles in the 'gunmetal' paint produces an oily sheen that can look most effective. If more paint needs to be shifted, add a little white spirit to the bud.

This Class 40 was rubbed gently with a fibreglass scratch brush before any paint was applied (only with vertical strokes) and this serves to produce a look of faded blue streaks. The 'brush-on-rub-off' method was then employed, before some delicate misting with an airbrush. All of this work adds far greater depth to a factory finish, portraying a machine with paintwork that has lasted over many years.

When I last saw the real 60044, the ageing blue livery was looking much the worse for wear. Whereas I wanted the blue Class 40 to have a faded and uneven finish, here I only wanted the livery embellishments to be worn away, so a little methylated spirit was applied and this works to gently soften the paint and any printed detail. Remove any excess fluid straight away and polish with a little 00000grade wire wool, if desired.

The site of 60044's former nameplates have been scarred by their removal so, after rubbing away much of the silver striping, a knife blade was used to scuff and scratch the paintwork around where the names used to sit. After applying a weathering coat by air – and hand-brush – the 'dirt' has remained within these scratches, as well as in the fine streaks created in the paintwork by the methylated spirit.

The exceptional grilles of the Hornby model can be enhanced by applying a little Tamiya 'gunmetal' to highlight the mesh. A similar effect can be achieved with a pencil lead or by 'dry-brushing' by hand with some Humbrol No.53 'gunmetal' enamel. The latter technique is achieved by dragging a flat brush lightly over the surface, having already removed all but the faintest traces of paint on to some tissue, and can be used to highlight any sort of raised detail. It's especially effective when using a slightly lighter mix of the base colour, such as blue on this model's side grilles.

The 'brush-on-rub-off' method need not be done by hand, but by airbrushing a wash of 'dirt' and then rubbing away the desired amount. A cotton bud will need to be slightly damp with white spirit to remove the much finer mist of paint, however. Whichever way it is done, the resulting streaks of dirt in and around doorways and grilles can look very effective, particularly when combined with a subtle spray of dust and smoke, plus some use of the Tamiya dry pigments to bring out the relief in the grilles. Don't forget to mask the windows first!

The depth of moulded grilles and louvers can be exaggerated by applying a wash of Tensocrom glaze with a fine brush, wiping away any excess with a damp cotton bud. These water-based paints dry to a slightly opaque finish that is much lighter than when first applied.

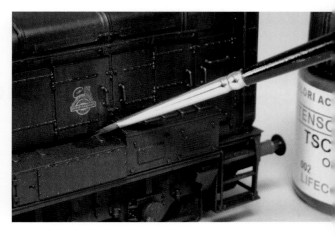

A degree of texture can be added to underframe areas by the addition of talcum powder to the weathering paint mix (acrylic or enamel). Adding a little gloss varnish here and there also helps, giving the illusion of wet or oily surfaces.

This Bachmann Class 08 has been airbrushed with acrylic weathering paints and it may be appreciated that these produce a slightly different finish to the enamels used in the previous projects. While I don't object to using water-based paint in this way, I find that the quality lies just beneath that of a good enamel. The Tensocrom glazes can be sprayed straight from the jar or brushed to create runs or streaks of leaking fluids, such as oil or diesel fuel, and can look very effective.

Weathering, in my opinion, forms one of the fundamentals of producing authentic-looking scale models. Key skills to acquire here are not only the application methods and the discernment of materials for specific tasks, but of using this knowledge and applying it appropriately, often with great care and restraint. It's often deceiving just how much gentle effort and painstaking work can go into both a gleaming, 'buffed-up' engine and a filthy, clapped-out machine desperately in need of some TLC.

Another way of achieving a pleasingly inconsistent base colour is to spray some fine streaks of a 'faded' shade, such as those offered in the Railmatch enamels range. Here, some 'faded' BR blue has been added over the Bachmann factory finish before the coats of dirt were applied.

CHAPTER 13

Cosmetic Surgery

Detailing and modifying ready-to-run locomotives not only encompasses refining what detail already exists or adding further enhancements, but sometimes it also involves correcting mistakes introduced to the product at source. Most errors are simply a matter of era-specific fitments or livery variations, while others may involve serious dimensional inconsistencies.

The ease of correcting such digressions varies according to the extent of each fault. Some modellers are willing to spend an inordinate amount of time and energy in search of perfection but I'm not one of these people, instead I'm more likely to realize that a compromise is required somewhere along the line and then plan my work accordingly. Working for a fast-moving magazine, with immovable print deadlines, means I've neither the time nor the inclination to spend months labouring over the same locomotive when, in most cases, it would simply be quicker to build one from scratch! This aside, I'm sometimes grateful for some of the minor errors introduced by manufacturers because it gives me something to do, and in the planning of a remedy can often spring the inspiration for a conversion project.

Bachmann's recent Class 47 was initially marred by the erroneous inclusion of reinforced windscreen surrounds, something more relevant to the re-engineered Class 57s. After removing the glazing, the frames can be quickly remedied by scraping away the raised bolt heads. Clean up with files and abrasive paper.

The underframe tanks also need a few modifications to correct detail errors. Firstly, cut away the moulded gauge dials (they're in the wrong place!) and instate replacements in the correct location by drilling a 1.5mm (1/16in) hole and inserting a length of 0.060in (1.5mm) rod. Push the rod so it sits just below the surface and then apply adhesive from the inside.

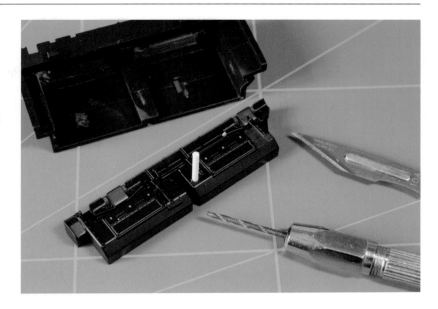

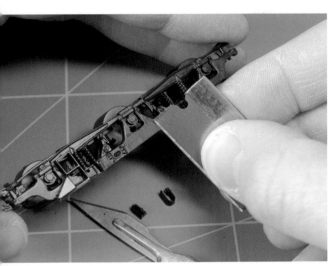

As has been the case with almost every Class 47 model released to date, the pipe runs along the top of the bogies have been included on all four frame faces. Looking at a 47 side-on (regardless of which side), only the left-hand bogie has these pipes. Cut away the offending items with a knife and/or scraper, tidying up any scratches with abrasive paper. Also remove the U-shape loops sited on one side, between the two frame beams.

With these modifications and a few other minor refinements, the Bachmann 47 proves to be an excellent model and offers various period-specific detail options.

Developing more of a discerning eye, as well as familiarizing oneself with the prototype in hand, should allow you to notice where a model has gone wrong. Couple this with an increased level of practical experience and knowledge of the products available (and suitability) and you should be able to plot a way forward. A handful of projects are suggested here and all can be undertaken without the need for much refinishing.

The art of instating missing seam lines is something that crops up from time to time and, although not involving any fancy tools or techniques, does require a high degree of accuracy and care. For most seams, a brand-new scalpel blade is the best tool for the job. Needle-point scribers could be used but I find that, no matter how sharp they are, they tend to have more of a dragging action rather than slicing to a clean edge. Clamping of the model into a vice is non-negotiable and the jaws should be padded to protect the paintwork without interfering with the level of grip. The straight edge, against which the blade will work, should also be clamped to the model if possible, leaving both hands free.

Only a couple of passes with the blade should be needed, moving slowly and with the barest amount of pressure, to guard against the knife wandering off-course. Keep the blade at a right angle to the model and, if the seam works around a curved surface, then pivot the blade over the contour, keeping part of it in contact with the straight edge at all times. In this instance, a long pattern of blade should be used, such as a Swann Morton No.11 or 16. As ever, maybe a trial run on a scrap loco or piece of rolling stock with a similar profile may be a good idea.

In most instances, the shallow knife-cuts should produce an acceptable finish with no other work required. However, if the cuts have to be made in several stages, or if there is any loose material clogging the crevice, the surface may be burnished with a toothbrush or with a soft polishing mop in a mini drill. Only use the latter method if you're familiar with the technique, as the difference between a perfect finish and blob of melted plastic is only a few seconds of contact!

On the Heljan Class 26, cutting through the light colours creates a distinct shadow within the knife-cut seam, promoting an authentic appearance. This isn't always so and cutting

Something missing from all Bachmann 'Peaks' until very recently was a representation of the distinctive horizontal seam, just beneath the top of the nose. Adding this is a straightforward task but accuracy is paramount, as fixing an error will require filling and repainting. After marking the location of the seam, mount the bodyshell into a vice and clamp a straight edge against the nose, protecting the paintwork with a strip of masking tape. With a brand-new scalpel blade, follow the edge very carefully, rotating the blade around the edges, whilst keeping it straight and level. A few passes should suffice.

A way of increasing the visibility of the seam line is to trail a small amount of dilute black acrylic paint into the recess, any excess being removed instantly with a damp cotton bud.

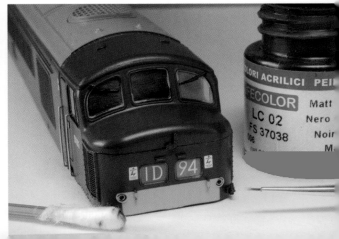

Here is the finished model with the effective nose seam.

A similar error plagues Heljan's otherwise excellent rendition of the Class 26 in its early guise; the front communicating doors have not been included, the prototypes not having them plated over until the 1970s. The same technique was employed to cut a series of vertical lines, but these were accompanied by some extra wire handrails and small hinges, cut from 0.010in square plastic strip.

into a plain green, as on the Class 46 (*see left*) does not have the same effect. Touching some weak black paint into the seam serves to exaggerate the depth but not necessarily the width. This is an important trick for use on some models, where making any cut into the paintwork exposes a brighter shade of the livery or a different colour entirely as bare plastic is revealed.

What projects such as these reveal is that no matter how many new models appear on the market, there are always facets of each traction type that are unrepresented, whether it be a true as-built Class 26 or a 37 with cast bogie frames. Of course, there are also more extreme variations within locomotive classes that are unlikely to be catered for in mainstream r-t-r releases; the following chapter highlights some of these.

RIGHT: A number of Class 37s received sets of cast bogies and this set is seen carrying 37706 whilst under overhaul.

BELOW: Whilst detailing a Vi-Trains' 37 (EWS-liveried 37405), I noticed that the real locomotive rides on a set of cast bogies, yet these have yet to feature on a r-t-r model, the only way forward being to modify a regular set. Cut away the raised beading around the frames with a sharp blade, without interfering with other details.

BELOW: I'm not keen on Vi-Trains' supplied bogie footsteps, so these brass replacements were assembled from a pack supplied by Craftsman Models.

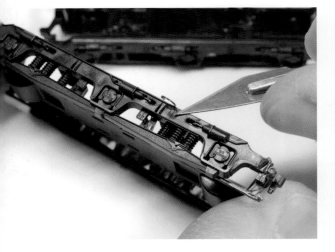

The modified bogie frames and new footsteps after painting and weathering.

Many refurbished Class 37s feature this pattern of fuel-tank level sensors, yet they don't appear on any r-t-r models.

The sensor is simply a piece of 0.060in (1.5mm) plastic rod and a short length of 0.3mm (30SWG) soft brass wire. Some sanding pipes were also added, in the same vein as those featured in Chapter 9, although this time they were secured into holes drilled alongside the moulded sanding valves in the top corners of the tanks.

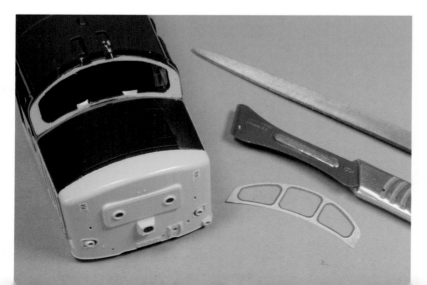

Some commentators have declared that the cab windows on the Vi-Trains' 37 are too large, so I endeavoured to remedy this by adding a brass overlay. A number of makers produce such products: this one is from the Craftsman range, but Shawplan and A1 also offer similar products. The glazing was removed and the area prepared.

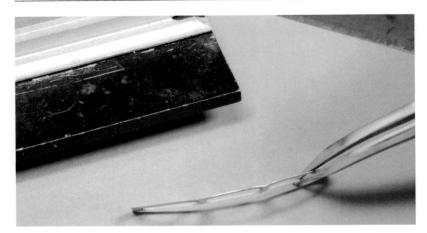

The brass overlay needs to be folded very gently to the distinctive profile of the prototype.

A fast-setting epoxy adhesive was used, the new surround being clamped with masking tape until set. Model filler was then spread around the new components and sanded to blend in to the rest of the bodywork.

The joy of liveries such as the sub-sector Railfreight scheme is that only the immediate area required priming and painting with an acrylic matt black and, after weathering, glazing was added. I'm still undecided about the success of this modification and I am yet to repeat it across my other Vi-Trains' models.

CHAPTER 14

What Money Can't Buy

Other than small-run or limited-edition commissions, there are models of certain prototypes that will probably remain unavailable for the foreseeable future. By this, I'm not referring to obscure locomotive types but production oddities or unusually modified members of so-called 'mainstream' diesel and electric designs that are already subjects of mass-production models.

Long-lived traction types, especially those designs that spawned huge fleets, enjoyed numerous scheduled refurbishment programmes and these are often catered for in the product ranges of most manufacturers. A good example is the Class 37 produced by Bachmann, that is available in 37/0 or 37/4 designations plus, a 37/5 is

also due to follow. What is unlikely, however, are models of Class 37s that received non-standard nose fittings or others with different patterns of headcode boxes at each end, both usually the results of collision repairs. Others still are known to have sported bodyside valances that had been cut much higher than usual during ad hoc maintenance work. Other locomotive classes would throw up a good number of stand-out individuals that add considerable interest to a model locomotive fleet but would be commercially unviable to produce.

There are also period-specific variations that are not currently offered in the r-t-r ranges. Many of these detail differences are relatively

The real 25168 received flush-welded panels in place of the former boiler compartment grilles that were usually just plated-over once the steam heating had been isolated. With some plastic card and plenty of model filler this is an easy feature to replicate, helped by the grille on the Bachmann model being a separate moulding and, therefore, it is easy to pop out. A new paint job is essential, though. There's no sign of a grille or a plate at the far end of this machine.

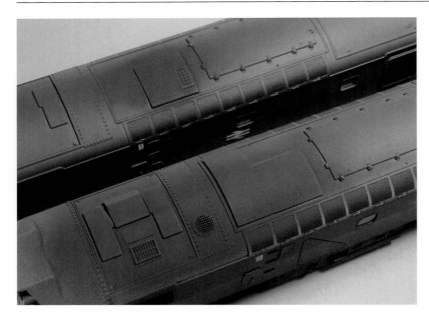

Some proprietary models are not available in original or early-life condition, so back-dating work must be done. For the Bachmann Class 25, moving the exhaust port back to the initial location involves removing the moulded rectangular port, extending the panel above the engine room hatch to an 'L' shape and then fitting a circular port within the adjacent narrow, riveted section. On this example (lower) a 5mm hole was drilled (working in 1mm increments) before being covered by an etched circular grille from A1 Models.

small but, without addressing them, an attempt to portray a model in as-built or early-life condition can be difficult. Such was the nature of BR's implementation of diesel and electric traction in the 1950–60s, that much of the research and development of these locomotives was carried out in service, rather than with proving prototypes on test trains. Consequently, an early production Class 25 diesel could, for instance, cover only a couple of years (or months in other cases) and r-t-r makers want a model that they can market as being suitable for as broad a period as possible.

Model designers do allow for some different options to be catered for, within one or more basic bodyshell toolings, with optional grilles or windows that can simply have the relevant parts clipped into place to suit the era and livery of the intended product, but even this approach has its limits.

A MAVERICK 'PEAK'

Ordered right at the beginning of BR's Modernization Plan, an initial batch of ten 2,300hp Type 4 locomotives was built at Derby,

entering service in 1959 and numbered D1 to D10 (later 44001/44010). The final two were fitted with heavy duty pressed steel grilles along both sides of the bodyshell and these looked markedly different to the carefully styled units as applied to the original eight machines.

A pack of suitable etched-brass components are in the A1 Models' range and simply require the model's moulded grilles to be removed. Cutting away raised detail on such a surface is not without its perils, as using a knife on such large areas can create a risk of the blade 'digging-in' and removing far too much material. Using a broad, flat file would remove this danger but a file is likely to damage other detail that must be retained. In this instance, I'd recommend using a single-edged scraper blade as produced by Expo Tools. If any readers are familiar with using a cabinet scraper to give a superior finish to a piece of wood, then the technique is virtually identical; the tool being gripped firmly between finger and thumb of both hands and the blade pulled over the surface. If the blade is fresh and sharp, waste material should be removed in fine shavings. As pressure is exerted on to the model, the deflection of the plastic body will affect the quality of

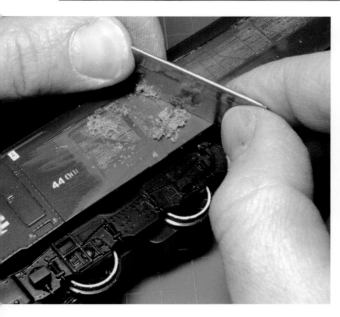

The final two Class 44s delivered to British Railways came fitted with American-style, heavy duty bodyside grilles and A1 Models offer a pack of etched grilles, but the original mouldings need scraping away first.

It's simple enough to fit the new grilles to the body. I doubt it's worth cutting holes in the shell to allow some daylight in, as the grilles are quite heavy and the perforations so narrow as to make it pointless. After filling any imperfections, prepare the roof fan aperture for a new grille, the edge of the moulding being retained, as was demonstrated on a Class 37 in Chapter 6. (See page 75.)

finish, so work with the chassis fixed in place and work steadily. Ideally, the surface should receive a quick rub-down with fine-grade abrasive paper to clear up any scratches.

I'd initially planned to drill-out and cut away some of the bodyshell to provide some depth behind the new grilles. However, after giving the matter some thought, I deemed it unneces-sary as the mesh is very fine and the brass quite thick; mimicking the heavy duty nature of the real things. Other than the use of the scraper, this project does not require any other technique that hasn't already been discussed, although the correction of the boiler compartment roof panels and the creation of the missing exhaust port provide a little scratchbuilding practice. Choosing the correct features to suit the model's intended period is especially pertinent here, as the original ten 'Peaks' had been cascaded to freight-only work by the late-1960s and certain

Embarking on this conversion also allows for a few discrepancies to be addressed, such as the lack of any exhaust port on this particular model (remedied on later Class 44 releases). Mark out the area and drill a pilot hole, enlarging with a square section needle file.

bits of kit, such as multiple working equipment and steam heating, were abolished.

My model (*see* below) represents 'Peak No.10', 44010 in mid-1970s condition, not far from retirement and with the Tryfan names removed. An interesting alternative would have been to choose D9/44009, as it wore the same heavy duty grille arrangement but, following an accident in 1969, it was subsequently rebuilt with a spare Class 46 cab at the No.1 end, featuring a single central headcode panel.

The exhaust port will look more authentic if some 0.010 × 0.020in (0.25 × 0.5mm) plastic strip is added. Fix in place, standing only slightly proud. When set, file down to match the roof profile but still a millimetre above the surface. Also, take the time to correct the panel arrangement over the boiler compartment, according to period. For this 1970s-era model, the boiler is no longer in use and the access hatch has been welded up.

The distinctive nose seam line also had to be instated (as in the previous chapter) before the model could be painted. Etched disc headcodes have been added along with correct bufferbeam detail to suit the period, i.e. no steam heat pipes or multiple working cables.

The homemade exhaust port is visible here and an authentic touch is the scratched paintwork where the *Tryfan* nameplates have been removed. The depth of the side grilles has been exaggerated by applying a wash of Tensocrom 'smoke' weathering pigment, from Lifecolor, brushed into the recesses and the outside immediately wiped clean.

AN ODDBALL 37

As hinted at in the opening of this chapter, the Class 37 represented one of the largest single locomotive types employed by BR and, with a career spanning nearly fifty years, plenty of 'off-beat' variations have appeared, even when considering the myriad batch differences and eventual sub-classes created by refurbishment.

Three of the original batch of 37s (37031, 37047 and 37053) had their split headcode boxes replaced with an unorthodox central panel, with marker lights set much closer together. This work was carried out at Plymouth Laira depot during the late-1980s and the engines gained a sort of 'cross-eyed' look. Furthermore, some features typical of 'split box' types, such as nose-mounted horns and strapping across the roof of the boiler compartment, were retained and 37047 – the subject of my model – also managed to keep its round buffers long after sister locomotives received oval replacements. (*See* below.)

Using a Vi-Trains' 37/0, already in the desired Mainline blue, as a starting point makes good use of the conveniently removable noses, making conversion work and refinishing much easier. Shawplan lens shrouds were employed over the plugged and re-drilled light apertures, taken from a pack of Class 37 marker light overlays. The same source provided the lovely etched horn grilles. Take care when creating the new lights as drilling to the final size straight away runs a risk of the bit wandering off. After the plastic rod plugs have been secured, mark the new locations (8.75mm apart) carefully and drill-out to the full

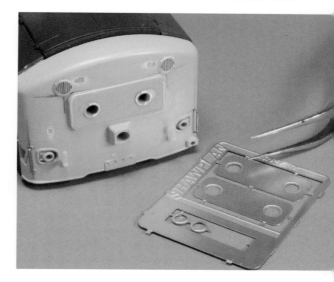

With such a numerous and long-lived locomotive type, such as the Class 37, there are bound to be a fair number of 'oddballs' with non-standard fittings and detail variations. This model portrays 37047, a former split headcode machine, fitted with centre marker light panels, yet with the lenses set closer together than was usual. The model's apertures were plugged with plastic rod and filler, then new holes drilled. Some etched lens shrouds were taken from a Shawplan pack.

size of 2.2mm incrementally. The factory-fitted lighting unit will need to be modified to suit the new lens positions, but take care when trimming the clear material that transmits the light to the lenses.

Other added details include rivet strips over the roof (Mainly Trains ref.MT163), etched horn grilles, extra nose-mounted handrails and round buffers. The recesses for the roof-mounted horns were filled and sanded smooth.

After re-numbering, patch-painting and weathering, a unique and distinctive Class 37 has entered into my fleet. Note the nearest underfloor tank that has been shorn of all moulded detail and been given a sharper lower edge to replicate conversion to a second fuel tank, a modification visited upon a number of Class 37s in the 1980s.

OLDER BOGIES FOR A CLASS 86

The 100-strong Class 86 formed the backbone of West Coast electric services from 1965 until the end of Virgin's use of the type in 2004. As originally built, the bogies were found to provide very unstable running qualities, especially at high speeds. Subsequently, a new design of suspension system was developed and Class 86s allocated to high-speed passenger and freight duties received the new equipment, as did the entire Class 87 fleet when built in the 1970s. Locomotives retaining the original pattern of bogies had various modifications carried out to improve matters, while the maximum speed was reduced to compensate.

Hornby's model of the Class 86 dates from 1981 and rides upon a set of the redesigned bogies with the characteristic large flexicoil springs and, thus, it can only accurately represent certain prototypes within a fixed period. A number of 86s still ran on original bogies into the 1980s and I can remember seeing them, hauling short-trip freights to and from Warrington. It was my aim to recreate one such loco, in late-1970s condition, thus the bogies had to be altered. Plenty of other detail had to be added, the model betraying

its age in a lot of respects. However, it does catch the look of the prototype and, once the effort has been put in, some very satisfactory results can be achieved.

There are many era-specific details to watch out for, aside from the bogies, such as different pantograph types, rooftop fire extinguishers and exhausters removed from the chassis on modern examples. Four-character headcodes or sealed marker lights and a choice of multiple working cables have adorned the cab fronts, along with large, square, high-intensity headlights or experimental small quartz lamps. Incidentally, the class was also built without the small sandbox doors in the cab sides, these being retro-fitted in the late-1960s.

Illustrated here are just a handful of project ideas, yet there are countless other possible routes to follow. Moreover, a quick trawl through any book, magazine article or internet site devoted to an individual locomotive type will reveal plenty of variations that won't be found in any r-t-r catalogue, be they minor fixtures or signs of heavy repairs. Certainly, if you want a model to stand out from the crowd – and not just in terms of quality craftsmanship – then producing something prototypically unique is well within your grasp.

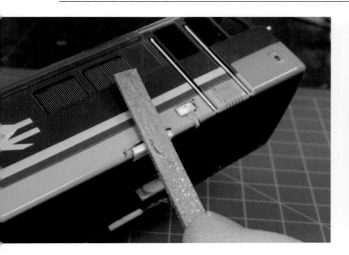

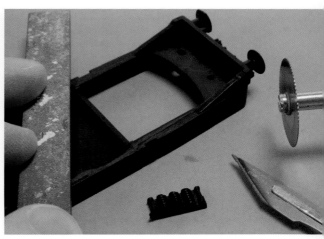

ABOVE: Hornby's Class 86 comes only in the form of a re-bogied example, yet some 86s lasted into the 1980s with the original pattern of underframes. To effect a conversion, the recesses in the body that accommodate the large flexicoil springs need filling-in with plastic strip and filler, then shaping to match the profile of the tumblehome.

ABOVE: The moulded springs should be cut away from the underframe and the surface flattened and smoothed with a file.

BELOW: The bogies themselves require some extensive surgery: cutting away the plinth for the large springs, reshaping the upper beam and resiting the hydraulic dampers

BELOW: Here, the twin dampers have been scratchbuilt from plastic rod and strip. Air piping, from nickel wire, runs along the top edge and the inverted triangular supports can be fabricated from 0.060in plastic angle. The moulded footsteps also require modifying to a tall, parallel form.

Detail work on the body is largely centred around the cab ends: handrails, buffers, lamp brackets, corner footsteps, multiple working cables (Heljan spares and nickel wire) and creating recessed door handles that were missing on this elderly second-hand model. The unsightly holes behind the cab doors that allow the chassis to clip to the body were also filled.

Once painted, the modified bogies should look the part. The body looks markedly better without the mounting clip holes and a pack of flushglazing replaces the moulded windows. The real 86008 lasted within the 86/0 sub-class, with its original pattern bogies, until conversion to an 86/4, 86408, in November 1985. Now numbered 86501, it is still in the hands of Freightliner.

Other than a new pantograph, obtained from DC Kits, the roof detail was left as supplied, although the large sliding pick-up switch was removed and the slot filled. The etched stainless steel BR symbol (also DC Kits) looks very effective on this model of 86008 portrayed as it was around 1978.

Focus on DRS

Direct Rail Services (DRS) was created in 1995 by its parent company British Nuclear Fuels Ltd (BNFL), in order to oversee the conveyance of material between its nuclear power stations and import facilities to Sellafield reprocessing facility in Cumbria. This traffic, along with the moving of necessary chemicals, had previously been handled by Transrail following the demise of British Rail. Based at Carlisle, DRS have since expanded into the intermodal and logistics market, as well as providing traction for test trains, railhead treatment or railtours.

A variety of locomotive types has been operated by DRS and they each offer the modeller some extraordinary detailing and modification

This view of a pair of DRS Class 37s illustrates some of the typical fittings that adorn refurbished locomotives: WIPAC light clusters, sealed former headcode boxes (right) or re-plated nose ends (left) and distinctive multiple working equipment. The two machines, 37069 and 37610, were working in multiple at Crewe in April 2004.

possibilities. The company began by assembling a modest but eclectic fleet of ex-BR 'heritage' diesel traction, rebuilding them in a manner unique to themselves. Plenty of variations in fitments, livery application and the unusual pairings of traction types ensure an enduring popularity with modellers and enthusiasts of the modern railway.

The first members of the motive power fleet were a batch of Class 20s, some of which dated back to 1959. These locomotives were comprehensively rebuilt and, although retaining the original power unit and equipment, were all fitted with up-to-date diagnostic equipment to increase reliability. The refurbishment programme also consisted of some drastic cosmetic alterations, most notably the removal of virtually all features from the nose and cab fronts. Group standard 'WIPAC' light units – that are now required to be fitted to all new-build mainline locomotives – were installed along with reinforced window frames and long range fuel tanks sited on the bonnet sides, immediately ahead of the cab. Multiple working cable receptacles were fitted to both ends but, unlike traditional practice, the actual jumper cables were stowed within the locomotive until needed. Some further, unmodified 20s were taken into stock and repainted in DRS colours but their use was only temporary.

As DRS expanded, so a fleet of Class 37s was assembled, along with a handful of Class 47s, each modified in slightly different ways. Experiments with various innovative traffic flows led to short-lived use of Classes 33 and 87. An initial batch of ten Class 66s was ordered in 2003, from General Motor's Canadian Electro Motive Division (EMD), followed by a further ten, three years later.

Class 47, 47802
Ready-to-run models of DRS machines have been numerous since the late-1990s, including more than a few Class 47s, possibly because most of these locomotives have not received as many cosmetic modifications as the Class 20s and 37s. My model of 47802 (overleaf) represents what is, I believe, the only member of the Class 47/8 sub-class to have retained the original cowling around the bufferbeams and the only real tell-tale DRS fitting is the recessed MU box on the cab front.

By working with a Lima model, I left myself open to having to fit many other details, such as new handrails, lamp brackets and radio aerials, the latter made up from 0.33mm wire and a strip of 0.010 × 0.020in (0.25 × 0.5mm) plastic. Brass oval buffers (A1) were set into etched buffer back plates with integral footsteps, which are from the Shawplan range, as are the brass marker light panel overlays. As mentioned in Chapter 13, some of the piping on the Class 47 bogies needs to be cut away. However, the type of plastic employed by Lima is not as easy to work with as that used on Bachmann models, and it can be difficult to achieve a smooth finish. Homemade speedometer and Heljan underframe tanks and battery boxes complete the detailing.

Suitable paint is available from Railmatch and Phoenix Precision paints, the attractive shade of blue being used across the DRS fleet. Transfer packs for DRS logos are only available via Lancaster City Models (see Appendix), as the company is very protective of its identity. The decals are produced to a very high standard and a proportion of each sale goes to help various DRS-endorsed charities. TOPS numbers and other embellishments have to be sourced separately, the likes of Fox or Modelmaster having a large selection of suitable packs.

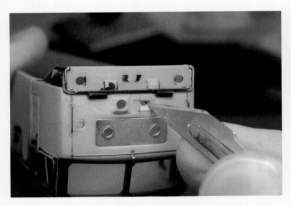

The Lima Class 47 requires much work to the cab ends in terms of basic detail enhancement and in adding a DRS multiple working (MU) receptacle. Mark the location and drill a 1.6mm hole, then use a sharp blade to create a square orifice.

The hole needs an angled backing, fitted from 0.010in (0.25mm) plastic cut to size and affixed from the inside. Then, 0.060in (1.5mm) rod and 0.010 × 0.020in (0.25 × 0.5mm) strip combine to form the cable junction box. A Pin Flow applicator delivers a tiny drop of adhesive to the delicate parts.

The site of the boiler exhaust on 47802 has long since been plated over and the moulded aperture should be filed and sanded away from the roof. The moulded twin radiator fan grilles were replaced with etched brass components (A1 Models).

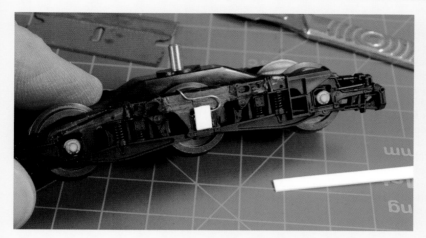

A speedometer can be assembled from 0.030 × 0.125in (0.75 × 3.2mm) plastic strip and some 0.3mm (30SWG) nickel wire, trimming the axle-box at a slight angle to give a flat surface and a better glue joint.

With all the details in place, including new underframe tanks and battery boxes from Heljan spares, the Class 47 is ready for its date with the DRS paint shop.

The new 'Compass' version of the DRS livery is an eye-catching scheme and these excellent transfers are only available through Lancaster City Models. The driver is just visible and he wears the correct uniform and DRS-branded 'hi-vis' vest!

Class 20, 20306

The lack of a fully-fledged refurbished DRS Class 20 in the r-t-r market makes it an ideal subject for a conversion project and, needless to say, quite a bit of work is needed to transform a standard Bachmann 20. Firstly, the cab and nose ends must be stripped of all projections and any recesses filled. This will probably take a few shots of putty and sanding to get a truly smooth surface upon which the new components will sit.

WIPAC light units are available variously as etched components from A1 and white-metal castings from Shawplan. I tried the etched pack on the cab end, having to build up a plastic backing for the thin pieces of brass, while the Shawplan castings sit on the nose end, raised up slightly from the edge of the running plate; this was meant to help me evaluate which was the better product, but each has its own merits.

Plastic strip and rod has been utilized for the MU fittings, these being of 0.060in (1.5mm) square section cut to an acute angle and adorned with slithers of 0.40in (1.00mm) rod for the connector, plus some 0.010 × 0.020in (0.25 × 0.5mm) for the hinge. Central headlights were cut from 0.090in (2.25mm) square strip, fixed in place and then marked and drilled to form the lens. The new window frames, etched-brass components from A1, reveal the original aperture frames to be larger than required, so scrap plastic strip was glued inside the openings and filler applied to tidy up the edges.

In parallel to the rebuilt prototypes, the Bachmann model requires a great deal of modification. Visible here is the filled and sanded flush end, radio roof pod, WIPAC light clusters (A1 Models), central headlamp, multiple working receptacle and new window frames (A1). To fit the new frames, the cab window apertures must be reduced in size, using plastic strip and filler.

The nose end must also be cleared of any detail and filled to a flush surface. Again, WIPAC lights (Shawplan at this end) are added and a centre headlamp, plus the MU connector. The opportunity may also be taken to replace the roof grille and bonnet handrails with finer parts.

Aside from the modified ends, the other notable addition is the pair of long-range fuel tanks sitting on each side. Assembled from plastic card, I had to surmise the dimensions from photographs, as I had no scale drawings to hand. Opting for tanks 22mm long and 12.5mm tall, I think they look about right. In fitting these tanks, a compromise has been made, as on the nearside of the bonnet (the left-hand side if looking toward the nose from the cab), the engine-room door immediately ahead of the new tank should have been replaced with a vented unit. This would mirror the opposite side, where a row of three vented doors are fitted. The extra airflow is required as the fuel tank has blocked part of the existing vents and this modification could have been attempted, either by scratchbuilding a set of horizontal shutters from plastic strip, or even by cutting the door away and dropping in another cut from a spare 20. Either way, it would be important to get it looking right. Sometimes you must decide whether a mediocre attempt to portray what should be there is preferable to leaving it be and not drawing attention to the area in question. Is this modelling heresy? If so, I can live with it.

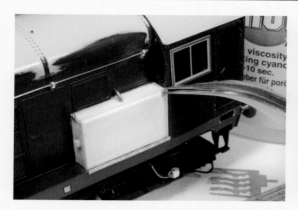

Long-range fuel tanks can be assembled from 0.030in (0.75mm) plastic card and any gaps sealed with model filler. A line of rivet detail was added along the bottom edge using the Mainly Trains pack of etched rivet strip (ref.MT163) and lifting lugs improvised by cutting up some scrap etched brake shoes. A fuel gauge sits on the forward edge of the tank, cut from 0.040in (1mm) rod.

A speedo is, again, a simple construction of 0.060in (1.5mm) square strip and some fine wire. On my chosen prototype, 20306, the bogie at the cab end sports a flush-sided lower equalizing beam and so the raised beading was cut away.

Wearing the original DRS scheme, 20306 looks rather different to the Class 20s as originally built.

The stark cab front contrasts with the original headcode fitments. Small washer jets can be discerned below the front windows, bent up from fine nickel wire.

CHAPTER 15

A New Set of Wheels

Unless a model is destined only for a display cabinet, having a level of mechanical performance to match the enhanced outward appearance is an obvious requirement. This is not such as issue with the majority of new locomotives produced during the past decade, fitted as they invariably are with a smooth, quiet and powerful centrally-mounted 'can' motor with twin flywheels and driveshafts, plus all-wheel power collection.

Bogie-mounted motor units, such as the infamous Lima 'pancake' or Hornby's Ringfield-type are confined to older products, although Hornby has updated this type of power unit within its own (and former Lima) models. These incorporate a five-pole magnet (in place of the former three-pole layout) and a skew-wound armature; these features enable smoother starting and running characteristics. The number of wheels collecting power is also increased on such upgraded products and this has a positive impact on performance.

Within this book, however, are a number of Lima and Hornby products that date back into the 1980s, either as long-standing members of my collection or recently acquired second-hand models. After lavishing so much attention to the cosmetic appearance, it seems foolish not to devote an equal amount of effort into ensuring that they run satisfactorily. There is nothing to say that an original motor should not be retained, provided that it is in good order and well maintained. Care for model motors entails regular cleaning and lubrication (although not to excess); this subject can't be entered into here in

too much depth, as it would fill a book in its own right. However, any model requires *all* of the following factors to be in place to ensure reliable running, regardless of the controlling method.

1. Well-laid, clean trackwork.
2. Clean wheels that are in-gauge and fitted 'true' to the axles.
3. Well-maintained, lubricated motor and gears.
4. Full electrical continuity to track and between wheels and motors of locomotives.

Track cleaning can be an onerous task at the best of times but there are few realistic short-cuts. Rolling stock with integrated cleaning gear is a good investment and keeping the wheels of everything that runs on your layout clean will help. Track-laying is probably the most important aspect of layout building because, if it isn't done properly, trains will never run reliably, no matter how clean the railheads are kept. Wheelsets should suit the type of track in use, i.e. finescale rail will not cope with the large flanges and wide profiles of older stock and a back-to-back gauge is always handy to check that wheels are riding on their axles properly and have not run 'out-of-gauge'.

The motor itself should be maintained according to any supplied instructions and these usually illustrate when and where to add lubrication. Use only specified model oils or greases and never over-lubricate as this can lead to contaminated armatures and create dirt on wheels and rails. Carbon brushes, found on old 'pancake' or

The trusty old Ringfield motor still lives on in certain, more senior, products in Hornby's catalogue. Now produced with a five-pole magnet and skew wound armature, performance is much smoother than in the past and all-wheel power collection is more common. However, the standard heavily flanged wheels still persist and this power unit from a Class 91 has received a set of Ultrascale drop-in replacements.

Something that rarely features on r-t-r locomotives is a rendition of bright steel brake discs fitted to appropriate models. This pack of etched stainless steel inserts, from Inter City Models, is designed specifically for the Lima/Hornby Class 67. Simply fix to the wheels with superglue and leave them shiny as per the real thing.

Ringfield units, can be popped out of the sprung retainers and checked regularly, especially if the model is run for long periods, as they tend to wear out. Ring magnets within old motors can benefit from being re-magnetized, as they can lose their power over time. A tell-tale sign of this is when a model requires significantly more current to be applied before it will move. There are a number of dealers who specialize in servicing and reconditioning motor units, and these can usually be found in the advertising pages of the railway press.

Testing for electrical continuity is best achieved with a multi-meter or other similar testing apparatus. Remember that checking only the soldered joints at each end of a wire is not sufficient, as a break can be hidden within the PVC insulation. Clean power-collecting surfaces are essential, as these can easily become clogged with detritus over time. Check also that any 'wiper'-type pickups are bearing on to the wheel or axle at all times, particularly if there is a degree of lateral movement in the axle.

A RE-ENGINEERING PROGRAMME

The obvious solution to a malfunctioning power unit is to replace it, either in a like-for-like manner or with a different, upgraded version. The ease with which this can be done is dependant on the model in question. Spare-part dealers can offer anything from a carbon brush spring to a complete motor bogie assembly for most Lima, Mainline, Dapol and (older) Hornby locomotives. Newer, high-specification models are not such an easy proposition, due mainly to the fact that they are not expected to wear out so readily. If problems arise with any such model, contact your local dealer or the manufacturer.

I've upgraded most of my older Hornby locomotives with the new five-pole motor and enhanced pickup arrangements and these are satisfactory for everyday operation. Some original Lima motors survive in use; the wild fluctuations in performance of the 'pancake' means that a few still run sweetly, while others were never any good and have received new 'drop-in' replacements. Such purpose-built upgrades are manufactured in Australia by a firm called ModelTorque and various units are offered for virtually all Lima OO models. Consisting of a replacement motor and integral mounting bracket, only the armature and ring magnet must be removed before the new unit can be screwed in place. A speed-reduction diode set is also provided to limit the motor's top speed to mirror that of the original. Happy with DC or DCC control, the unit offers an increased torque output, thus requiring a lower starting voltage and drawing less current throughout the speed range.

If your old Lima 'pancake' mechanism is misbehaving, it may be time to retire it in favour of a made-to-measure replacement that re-uses the motor housing and gears. Dismantle the Lima unit by removing the two screws on the face of the housing, taking out the sprung carbon brushes and pulling away the armature. The ring magnet must also be levered out.

Remove the two small bolts that retain the plastic gears and strip all parts, putting them to one side. This may also be a good opportunity to replace the wheels with their enormous flanges! Pull the wheel from its axle with pliers.

The motor housing, gears and brass pickup contacts can now be given a thorough clean with a solvent. I used an aerosol airbrush cleaner, used sparingly, as it evaporates quickly and cleanly rather than something like WD40 that leaves behind an unnecessary residue.

The new Ultrascale wheels drop-in to the motor bogie in the same way as illustrated on page 166 and the gears can be refitted, checking that everything turns sweetly. Push the ModelTorque motor into the housing, drive gear end first, then loosely refit the two original screws.

A brass bearing is supplied to fit into the drive gear housing and the motor's shaft should sit exactly central inside this. There is room for adjustment in the mounting screw holes as long as they are not screwed tight.

Once happy with the alignment of the motor's shaft, tighten the two mounting screws. Gently push the motor along a flat surface and check that everything is turning freely.

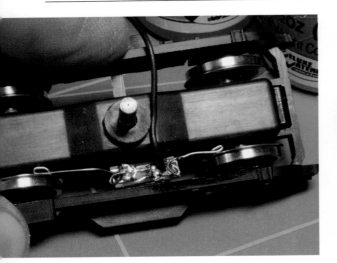

Adding extra pickups will always improve performance on older models, and this Lima Class 87's unpowered bogie has had an extra set of contacts added. A length of copper 'spring' wire is soldered to a small scrap of copper-clad board, which in turn is epoxied to the bogie frame. A length of wire links to the motor bogie and the copper wires should rest gently against the inside rims of the wheels. However, make sure that the pickup acts on the correct wheels! The right-hand rail, when viewed from the driver's cab of the unpowered end, is positive for forward movement so this assembly should be on the left-hand side when looking forward.

The ModelTorque motor is supplied with a diode assembly (seen in the pink insulation cover) which limits the motor's top speed to a more realistic value. Make all necessary connections and then test run for about half an hour in each direction, preferably on a rolling road.

Combining the fitting of one of these power units with some extra pickups and, maybe, a new set of wheels, enhances performance markedly. New wheelsets are discussed later, but the opportunity should also be taken to strip the gears and existing power-collecting components for a thorough clean and degreasing. Although the motors are easy to fit, care must be taken to align the final drive properly and to achieve an accurate meshing with the nylon gears. Check for smooth running by pushing the bogie along by hand and feel for any 'tight' spots.

ModelTorque have also developed a replacement motor and transmission system that is intended to replace centrally-mounted 'can'

motors. Automatic Torque Control (ATC) units look similar to a standard motor and flywheel assembly but each brass flywheel is actually two separate units, constituting a torque transfer box. In this sense, the motor is not directly connected to the wheels and the amount of torque produced varies according to the demands being placed on the locomotive in terms of load, gradient and speed. Motor stalling is thus eliminated and the model is provided with an increased level of operational realism.

SELF-CONTAINED MOTOR BOGIES

The Black Beetle range of four-wheel power bogies, each consist of a small Mashima motor powering both axles via a set of brass gears and a horizontal drive shaft. Equipped with electrical pickups, these Australian-built units are also available as matching 'dummy' bogies, all in a vast array of wheelbase options ranging from 25.5mm to 40mm (in increments of 0.25mm).

Nickel silver wheels are fitted and various wheel diameters catered for, from 9.6mm to 14mm in spoke or disc form. Designed primarily for railmotors or multiple units, they can also be fitted beneath locomotives, although a pair will be required to tow anything more than a couple of carriages. Most of the more popular wheel options are held in stock by suppliers such as DC Kits, but other options can be built to order.

Illustrated below is the fitting of a 36mm wheelbase Black Beetle to an elderly Lima 0-4-0 shunting locomotive, taken from my first train-set, back in the early 1980s. The original Lima 'pancake' hadn't worked for years but, with a suitable amount of ballast within the bodyshell, the new motor copes well with the demands placed upon it whilst shunting my small layout based in an Allied railway yard during the War. Compensation is achieved by the slight flexibility of a home-made brass cradle and a central pivot allows for a degree of vertical deflection. A controlled amount of lateral movement is also achieved by the fixing of coil springs to either side of the unit, acting against the central bracket of the motor housing. The springs were taken from a pack intended to mount pickups on to an electric guitar and are rather stiff, especially

when cut to a shorter length. Compensating the chassis enhances the road-holding qualities and, thus, greatly improves power collection.

Working on a similar format to the Black Beetle is the BullAnt range. The highly-regarded Mashima motor is again incorporated, although it is mounted in a higher position and fitted with a brass flywheel for smoother performance, especially at slow speeds. The drive shaft drives through a vertical reduction gearbox, transmitting power to each axle via a horizontal shaft. Other than excellent performance, the great benefit of the BullAnt is the virtually endless wheelbase options available between 14mm and 60mm, in 2-, 3- or 4-axle versions. Indeed, units can be custom-built to suit almost any prototype and include a choice of motor and gear combinations. Again, dummy units are also available, all with phosphor bronze 'wiper'-type pickups.

Both the Black Beetle and BullAnt units come supplied with plastic brackets for the mounting of appropriate bogie sideframes; there are various methods of fixing them to a locomotive's chassis, depending on the prototype. Black Beetles incorporate a central pivot screw, so a

Black Beetle motor bogies are completely self-contained motor and gearbox assemblies, available in a range of wheelbase and wheel type/size configurations. All that's needed is something for the unit to pivot from. In this case, an old Lima 0-4-0 diesel shunter, the chassis has been cut to accept the new motor while a strip of 0.030in brass has been marked out to form a cradle.

The brass has been folded to shape and drilled to accept the motor's mounting screw and the securing bolts from the chassis. As a way of controlling lateral movement, two short lengths of a stiff coil spring have been glued either side of the unit, acting against the side supports of the motor's casing. This, along with the vertical pivoting of the cradle mount gives this small loco a good degree of compensation and this will improve its running and power collecting performance.

Motorbogies.com offer a bespoke service, assembling 'BullAnt' motorized and trailing bogies to your own specifications. Mashima flywheel-fitted motors are fitted, connected to a reduction gearbox and driveshaft to power all axles on the bogie. Trailing bogies have pickups fully set-up and ready to connect to the motor.

suitable bracket must be provided, fashioned from brass or plastic. On the other hand, the design of the BullAnt means that the position of the motor precludes a similar fixing, although a choice of pivot arms and brackets exist and these can be tailored to suit different situations.

Another alternative powered bogie is the super smooth Halling motor bogie, again designed with the multiple unit or locomotive in mind. The motor sits centrally and is fitted with a pair of brass flywheels and can be supplied with a choice of disc or spoked wheels (in various diameters) and with either an adjustable or fixed wheelbase, although only in four-wheel configurations. The Tenshodo 'Spud' is well-known as a reliable motor bogie, but its use is better suited to lightweight railcars or multiple units. Additionally, Branchlines offer a Bo-Bo motor bogie kit that can be built into a powerful and smooth-running unit for railcars or locomotives. Supplied as a set of fold-up nickel silver etched parts, a Mashima motor drives a lay shaft, via an overall gear reduction of 30:1. As it is only available with a wheelbase of 55mm, this is an inflexible option compared to the other products, but is worth investigating nonetheless.

All of the units mentioned here are reasonably priced, even the custom-built BullAnts, although it should be factored into your plans that these can take a few months to arrive. Incidentally, the BullAnt range also offers a kit for a centrally-mounted, cardan shaft-driven motor assembly and chassis. More details can be found on the Motorbogies.com website listed in the Appendix.

RE-WHEELING

Apart from looking much more attractive and authentic, a finely crafted set of wheels can also improve power collection and riding characteristics. It goes without saying that newer locomotive releases have, by and large, much better

After expending so much time and energy on super-detailing this Lima Class 87, it seems natural to continue by upgrading the mechanical aspects, too. A new motor and new wheelsets bring this 30-year-old model up to date.

wheelsets than earlier products but, depending on your modelling standards in terms of track and stock, there is always room for improvement with mass-produced equipment.

Most modern OO-gauge r-t-r motive power is now fitted with wheels that comply to the National Model Railroad Association (NMRA) Recommended Practice 'RP25' profile of wheel tread and flange. The dimensions that were set down in this 1997-dated classification are calculated to be the optimum for road holding and prototypical appearance within what is practicable to suit NMRA-conforming track. As track can be built in varying specifications, a range of variables are set out in the 'RP25' document to compensate and, hence, we have codes that relate to the actual dimensions of the wheel contour; the smaller the code, the smaller the wheel. In practical terms, a Code 110 wheel is accepted as a 'standard' for users of most contemporary model railway track systems, most notably Peco's Code 100 rail. Modellers utilizing 'finescale' track, such as Code 75 or 55, are recommended to try Code 88 wheels, whose finer profile and smaller flanges look much more effective.

All of these codes can make your head hurt but, whether the model's wheels conform to the 'RP25' specification or not, another oft-employed r-t-r compromise is in the use of under-sized wheels, in terms of overall diameter. This is done to allow the bogies free rotation around tight curves without the flanges scraping the underside of the bodyshell. Most people will not even notice this imperfection but on some models the 'look' of the machine can be influenced, although if there are tightly curved rails on your layout then such wheels cannot easily be replaced.

Naturally, older models invariably feature wheels with larger flanges and wider tread surfaces and their use on modern track (Code 75 and sometimes even 100) can lead to short-circuits or derailments when crossing through pointwork and, in extreme cases, the flanges can actually foul the sleepers or rail chairs. Across the board, then, there is scope for the replacement of a locomotive's wheelsets to suit particular needs.

The aforementioned Black Beetle and BullAnt motor bogies can be obtained with either Code 110 or 88 wheel profiles, as can the Branchlines power unit kit. Moreover, the latter firm can offer the high-quality Black Beetle wheels alone for use in specific r-t-r locomotives and multiple units in place of the originals.

As for 'drop-in' replacement wheels, probably the most comprehensive range is offered by Ultrascale, whose expansive catalogue includes a choice of general packs designed to be a straight swap for the most common chassis employed by Lima and Hornby, in 4- or 6-axle sets. Typically, the dummy bogie wheels are ready assembled on their axles and do, literally, drop into place. Driving wheels, however, will require assembly after slotting the axles through the bearings. Finely rendered brass gears are incorporated to the wheels, where necessary, and the use of a back-to-back gauge is essential for accurate fitting of wheels on to the axle.

Ultrascale also offer bespoke packs for more recent models, from each of the main manufacturers, providing finer profiles and a more prototypical wheel pattern. Older models, such as those by Mainline, Dapol and Airfix, are also catered for. All wheels are available in either nickel silver or

Ultrascale offer packs of wheels and axles designed specifically for a range of r-t-r locomotives. This set is for the Hornby Class 92 and the unpowered bogie wheels are already set and gauged on the axles, so are a simple drop fit into the chassis block, ensuring the pick up contacts bear against the inside rim.

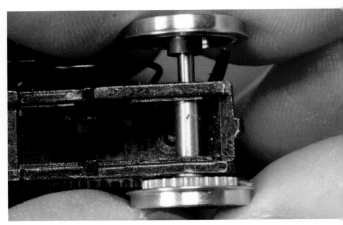

To remove the Hornby wheelset from the motor housing, either pull apart by hand or use a pair of pliers to part one wheel from the axle.

Insert the part-assembled Ultrascale set into the bearing slot, ensuring the gear wheel is on the correct side. Then push the other wheel on to the axle carefully but firmly. Use a back-to-back gauge to set the distance between the inner faces of the wheels (available from Mainly Trains).

brass and are supplied in a bright polished finish that benefits from priming and painting (outer faces only) or from the use of chemical blackening fluids such as Carrs Metal Black.

A look at the photographs of the Hornby Class 92 and Lima Class 87 (below and page 164) illustrate the enormous impact that a finer set of wheels can make upon a model locomotive. Do these extra bits of engineering not make each

exercise expensive? The Class 87 was obtained second-hand for £25, the new motor cost about the same again and the wheelsets set me back £15 (all at 2007 prices). Add an extra 'tenner' for detailing parts and a figure of £75 is reached; less than the rrp of most new r-t-r diesel and electric outline models.

The finished Hornby Class 92 with an Ultrascale set of wheels. The finer profile offers a drastic improvement and allows the loco to better negotiate finescale track and pointwork.

CHAPTER 16

Light Fantastic

Working head and tail lights are now an integral part of many contemporary ready-to-run locomotives and it follows, therefore, that the retro-fitting of lighting units to other stock would be a logical step towards harmonizing a motive power fleet. There are certainly plenty of off-the-peg lighting units available within the model railway trade, most sets being tailored to specific products in the Lima, Hornby and Bachmann ranges. These products not only cater for models that lack factory-fitted lights but also aim to enhance some of the more basic arrangements on products such as the Hornby Class 92, ex-Dapol Class 56 or Lima HST power car.

A couple of non-DCC products are featured in this chapter and they represent two different approaches: a ready-made drop-in unit for a specific prototype, and a kit of parts adaptable for fitting to almost any locomotive. There is, however, a wider range of lighting solutions on the market and a brief search across the internet or through the advertising pages of the modelling press will proffer some interesting leads.

Whatever lighting system is chosen, there are some common variables to consider. Most commonly, the new components fitted to the inside of the bodyshell may interfere with the refitting of the chassis and some material will have to be cut away. When doing this, take a moment to check that the underframe will not be seriously weakened by removing too much plastic. Of course, if fitting a kit for a particular model, the instructions should provide suggestions of how best to proceed.

Additionally, applying black paint on to the inner surface of the bodyshell around where lights are to be fitted is a key step. Without doing so, the glow from the bulbs or LEDs will spread across the lightly-coloured plastic. If a deep aperture is used, such as for a BR standard high intensity headlamp, it would be advantageous to paint inside the walls of this, for the same reason.

One final point to consider is the removal of any factory-fitted lighting unit and, in particular, the clear plastic 'lens' that is often used to reflect light from a single bulb to two or more apertures on the cab front. As the illustrations of the Class 67 show (overleaf), these units can sometimes be glued fast to the bodyshell, making safe removal very difficult. The use of a cutting burr in a mini power-drill is probably the quickest and safest way of dealing with this, as just the necessary areas can be cleared and the rest left in situ.

FITTING A 'LIGHT STORE'

Express Models of Loughborough offer an amazing range of light-based products for model railways, be it flashing neon signs or an arc-welding machine. One of their most innovative, however, is the 'Light Store' unit, available for specific r-t-r locomotives, carriages and multiple units. Consisting of a bank of capacitors, the circuitry accumulates stored power whilst the train is running and, once the locomotive comes to a halt, this back-up source is tapped into. Thus, the head and tail lights can remain illuminated for up to a few minutes.

As the circuitry and LEDs are all ready-assembled, the act of fitting each unit requires

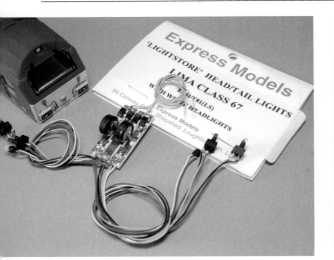

Supplied ready assembled, the lighting units from Express Models are probably the easiest to fit, needing only the drilling of suitable holes and connection to the power supply. This 'Light Store' version contains an array of capacitors that gather power as the train is running and then uses it to keep the lamps lit when the loco comes to a halt.

This pack has been designed for the Lima/Hornby Class 67 and holes are required for the lenses: 2.5mm for the main headlights and 2mm for the marker lights. The basic factory-fitted lighting should be discarded and the clear plastic removed. I found this difficult on my model, so firmly was it glued to the body, so a burr in a mini drill was used to carefully grind away the excess material before drilling the necessary holes.

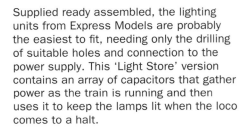

only the two power-feed wires to be soldered to the locomotive's pickups, plus the drilling of holes for the lights to sit in their apertures. A good set of instructions are included with each kit and they are available for a good many Lima, Hornby, Heljan and Bachmann models. In drilling the holes through the moulded light units,

be sure to mark the centre carefully with a sharp point before using the drill and open the holes in increments to ensure an accurate job.

The advantages of using this system are largely self-evident, but the difference in intensity of the main headlight and marker lights is satisfyingly realistic. The level of brightness remains

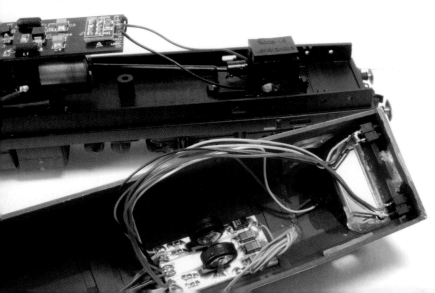

After painting the interior of the cabs with a couple of coats of acrylic black, the lights were pushed into place.

unaffected, regardless of how much power is being applied – an area where older lighting circuits fail. Fitting is very straightforward, as has been suggested, although some problems may be encountered on other models, where more chassis or cab interior moulding material may need cutting away to provide adequate space. This Class 67 project, by the way, took about 45min to complete.

The only drawback of this system becomes evident when changing the modified locomotive's direction or using it for shunting manoeuvres. Needless to say, the stored power keeps the white headlights burning whilst the red tail lenses light up and vice versa. In view of this, it may be wise to consider what duties a loco is likely to perform on your layout before opting to fit such a unit.

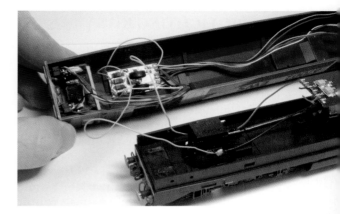

The circuit board is supplied with a double-sided sticky pad to enable it to be fixed to the underside of the roof at a point where it will not impede the motor assembly. Solder the two power lines to the pickup collector points on the nearest bogie unit and check that the polarity is correct (e.g. white lights showing at the front end) and, if not, swap the wires.

With the model reassembled, the lights should look very effective, the main headlight having a brighter intensity than the markers.

The red tail lights are equally as impressive and the 'light store' feature adds an interesting touch to non-DCC layouts.

GENERIC LIGHTING KITS

A different approach to a tailor-made solution is the use of a more generic set of parts that can be fitted to virtually any desired locomotive. First Class Trains offer a modern traction lighting kit that is suitable for any machine fitted with a high-intensity headlight and separate marker/tail lights; encompassing most of BR's mainline fleet in post-1980 condition.

In the kit is a set of eight small LEDs to form the marker and tail lamps, plus two larger white LEDs for the main headlights. A small pair of pre-wired circuit boards contains the necessary diode assemblies to control the flow of current through each set of lights and lengths of red and black wire. As this is a kit, much more soldering is required and, as the LEDs are soldered together after fixing into the bodyshell, some prior experience with an iron is desired.

By closely following the supplied wiring diagrams, the task is not too onerous, as long as the long and short LED leads are correctly oriented whilst being set into the cab fronts, using epoxy glue. Push the lenses into the drilled-out holes and then smear the adhesive around the base and hold until set. Any glue clogging the aperture or smeared on the lens will impair performance. Once all the bulbs are in position and the epoxy hardened, the leads can be soldered together in the prescribed order and the diodes connected into the circuits. It's crucial to get everything connected correctly first time, as making corrections, as I had to, can be difficult and frustrating.

Checking the wiring with a battery saves a lot of hassle and helps to identify any mistakes at an early stage. Once everything is working properly, insulate all the joints carefully and ensure as many of the bare contacts are sealed as possible, to guard against short-circuits in future. Make any modifications to the chassis to allow it to fit and reassemble.

Fitting this kit to a Lima Class 47 took longer than the earlier project, not least due to my lapses in concentration. However, the results are greatly satisfying. As with the Express Models unit, the disparity in brightness between the main headlight and the more yellowish marker lights is correct and the vividness of all lights remains constant throughout the speed range.

Other generic lighting kits, such as this pack from First Class Trains, provide all the raw materials of bulbs, cable and diode assemblies. However, it's up to the modeller to adapt the components to the model at hand.

Following the kit's recommendations, I drilled-out the light apertures and glued the bulbs into place with a quick setting epoxy. This followed painting the inside of the cabs black to prevent the light 'bleeding' through the plastic. As the lights are all LEDs, the correct orientation of the two leads is essential as current can only pass through the components in one direction.

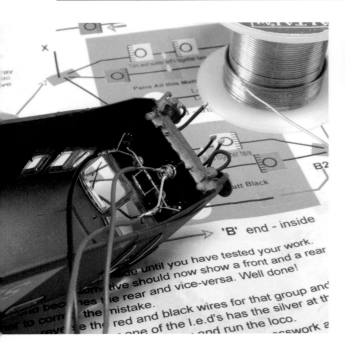

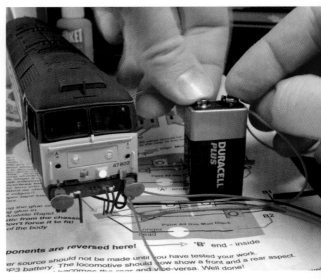

Following the kit's wiring instructions, solder the bulb leads together in the correct combination, then add the red and black wires to the diode assemblies.

Use a 9V battery to test the circuits, the two power supply wires being held against the terminals. Check that only the head or tail lamps are illuminated at one end at a time, reversing the wires on the terminals. If something's amiss then recheck everything against the wiring instructions.

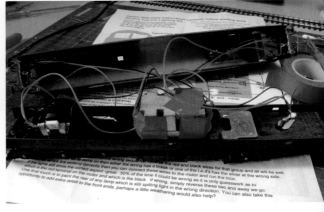

If everything is working correctly then add some heat shrink tubing or insulating tape to the exposed connections as this will prevent any short circuits.

Connect the two power leads to the motor's pickups, checking for the correct polarity by trial and error; you have a 50/50 chance of being right first time! Then tidy up all the wiring before fitting the body to the chassis.

A bright white headlamp and yellowish marker lights look just the job on this Lima Class 47 . . .

. . . and the tail lamps work too!

Both of these products offer their own distinct advantages and disadvantages and, as with anything else, putting some prior thought into what you're looking for in a lighting unit, before purchasing, will be well rewarded. These two locomotives now offer me different options for my layout and their performance is certainly equal to the latest 'high spec' models that work alongside. Indeed, they actually look better than some of them!

Throughout this book we have been addressing the idea of showing a high degree of attention to detail, in terms of observing correct representations of locomotive livery, fittings and equipment, specific to periods and prototypes. Add an improved mechanical performance and the only scope for further enhancement lies in adding realistic lighting.

CHAPTER 17

Born Again?

This final chapter is offered as something of an epilogue or, rather, an amalgam of all the techniques so far described, in an effort to transform a derelict, 30-year-old model to a useful, yet innocuous, member of my locomotive fleet. Being a sentimental old fool, there are some models that I keep hidden away that I could never bring myself to dispose of, even if it means a complete re-build. Moreover, sometimes I'd rather strive to make good use of what I already have, rather than freely spending money on new things.

Maybe my sentimentality is caught up in the thriftiness mentioned at the beginning of this volume or, maybe, I'm just tight-fisted. Either way, setting oneself a challenge and seeing it through to a conclusion is good for the soul, and I can guarantee that some valuable skills will be learned along the way. Incidentally, after recently featuring an article in *Model Rail* on the topic of updating a handful of Hornby and Lima Class 47s, the feedback that I received was far more voluminous than almost anything else I have covered in the past. There must be a few modellers out there who share an attachment to some of the more 'senior' models and a conviction as to their potential.

New meets old . . . the Hornby Class 37 model (right) dates from 1966 and, save for some cosmetic and mechanical refinements, has remained largely unchanged. When viewed alongside a Bachmann 37 from 2006, the different levels of detail and accuracy are apparent.

HORNBY CLASS 37:
SCRAP OR SALVAGE?

I can remember vividly the day I bought my first OO-gauge Class 37, having saved my pocket money for months. At that time, Lima had yet to offer its slightly refined alternative to the venerable Hornby product that harked back to the mid-1960s. As my modest budget of the time did not extend to new models, virtually all of my stock (and track) was purchased second-hand. This would often frustrate me, not because of any ideas of status, but for reasons of unpredictable mechanical performance. The crude representations of livery and detail features would also offend my eye, even from a young age!

My father's supreme renditions of Napoleonic or Prussian cavalry, using proprietary kits as a basis for super-detailed miniatures, spurred me to improve these old railway models and it was, perhaps, because my stock was mostly second-hand that I felt confident enough to take a knife and a paintbrush to it, without worrying about making expensive mistakes. Indeed, many of

my purchases were made with this is mind; the scruffiest or damaged item in the 'bargain bins' would be first considered, as long as the motor worked.

The Hornby Class 37 featured below dates from an early-1980s 'production run and, I seem to remember, carried BR blue with TOPS numbers. It was bought with the intention of applying the brand-new 'Railfreight red stripe' scheme that had just appeared. This I did, followed later by the triple-grey, sub-sector freight livery before it reverted to BR blue, sometime around 1990. Levels of detailing also changed over the years with flush-glazing being fitted from the offing, followed by various attempts at lamp brackets, handrails and buffer-beam fittings. A new motor was added at some point, bought reconditioned from a Hornby spares' dealer and some cardboard cab interiors also featured.

So, you see, this model has a history and explains why the thought of casting it out into oblivion is abhorrent. However, just how could it be brought up to a modern standard? Firstly,

Being a sentimental old fool, there are some models hidden away in my attic that I simply can't part with. I can remember vividly the day I bought this Hornby Class 37, having saved my pocket money for months. Surely there was some way of reprising this veteran of the Dent fleet?

Bachmann's original 37, released in 2003, contained some dimensional errors and, to its credit, the firm endeavoured to address these issues and produced a splendid follow-up 3 years later. I had a scrap original-release 37 bodyshell lying around and wondered about the viability of creating a hybrid model.

something would have to be done about the incorrect pattern of bogies, plus the nose ends and cab windscreens do not look 'right'. In fact, a list of potential improvements became very long! A catalyst for progress, however, came after constructing a model of a GWR gas turbine locomotive that required a Bachmann Class 37 chassis, leaving a spare bodyshell from which to take some 'spares'.

As the photographs on pages 175–181 show, a lot of work went into the project, centred largely on the body and, I think, has been worthwhile. The new wheelsets and bogie frames make a huge difference although, because of the shorter wheelbase of the Hornby motor and bogie, plus

the method of mounting, the wheel centres are not strictly accurate in terms of alignment with the body. In some instances, such things can be disguised, but here it results in a gap between the front of the bogie and the bufferbeam and a cramped central fuel-tank area. I took a reactive approach to this as I'd not realized the discrepancy early enough. Instead, a modified arrangement would have been sought. I can live with it for now and the fitting of snowploughs takes the attention away from the unsightly gaps but, who knows, maybe I'll revisit this model with a custom-built motor and chassis unit. There are a couple of areas of bodywork that could be tweaked as well.

The plan was to incorporate the better features of each, yet retain most of the Hornby model that I was so attached to, in an effort to create one acceptable 37; first step was to remove the least desirable aspects of the old bodyshell.

Nose ends, radiator side grilles, exhaust panels and fuel tanks were taken from the Bachmann product and fixed into the Hornby shell, reinforced internally with plastic strip where necessary.

One of the inconsistencies of the older Bachmann 37 was a nose section that appeared a little 'squat' in appearance and, when the ends are married on to a Hornby shell, the excess width is revealed. A compromise between the two was needed and use of filler and a flat file aimed to bring about a seamless joint and correct-looking profile.

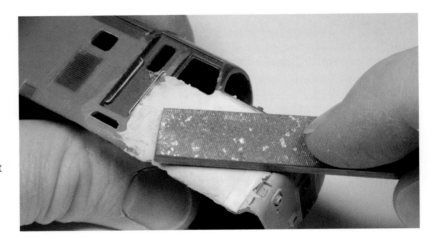

To achieve the distinctive tumblehome along the bottom of the body, some plastic strip reinforced the inside of the lower edge. Additionally, the Hornby chassis was modified and glued in place at this point to support the bodyshell whilst shaping work progresses.

With masking tape as a guide, a flat file formed the tumblehome, checking to ensure that the angle is consistent along the sides. The profile changes to a slightly more vertical plane between the cab doors and the bufferbeams. Careful study of the real thing was required to appreciate the subtle changes.

Having marked out the panel locations along the sides, a sharp needle point scriber and blade rendered this detail, along with the engine room access door.

The Bachmann exhaust panel and radiator side grilles were fitted into suitable apertures, with any necessary filling carried out with putty or plastic strip. Some Shawplan Mark 1 coach fittings were utilized to represent the engine hatch handles.

Plenty of etched components from the Shawplan, A1 and Craftsman Models ranges were utilized, along with the bufferbeams of the scrapped Bachmann Class 37.

A full set of side grilles are available from A1 Models, the mouldings having been cut flush. According to period, some of the bodyside steps should be filled in and the cantrail-level grilles require modifying to the correct pattern using filler and a scriber.

The boiler compartment roof needs the relevant exhaust or blanking plate fitting and I also represented the four distinct lifting lugs by setting some short lengths of 0.33mm wire into drilled holes. After supergluing in place, the wire was trimmed and filed to a uniform height.

The etched windscreen panels were assembled and fitted in the same manner as described in Chapter 13, but new channels had to be cut to accommodate the white-metal air horns. Waste material was drilled and cut, before fillets of plastic strip were fixed into place from underneath.

Other missing or damaged rivet detail was reinstated with short lengths of wire fixed into drilled holes, seen here around the radiator grille panel. A coat of grey primer will highlight any blemishes or areas that the filler has missed, so always treat the first few coats of undercoat as part of the preparation process.

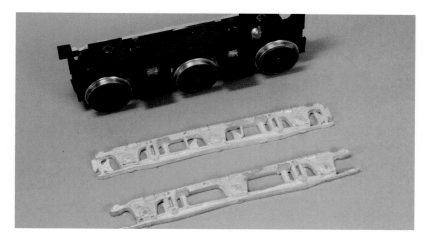

Although using a new Hornby five-pole mechanism, new Ultrascale wheels were fitted and the incorrect bogie frames cut away. Replacement white-metal castings, from the Alexander Models range, represent a set of cast frames with which 37424 ran from the late 1980s.

Plastic brake blocks must also be added, these being cut from the scarp Bachmann frames and a set of Craftsman brass footsteps were assembled and fitted, ensuring their location aligned with the cab doors.

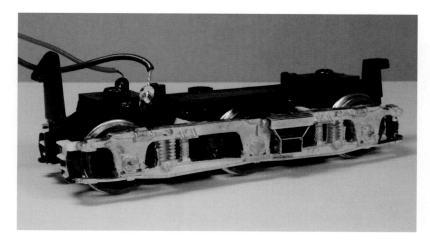

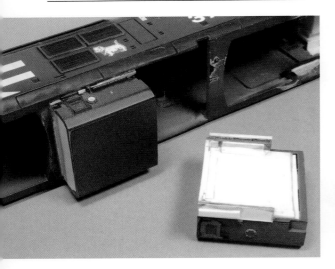

LEFT: The wheelbase of the Hornby bogies is a few millimetres too long, impacting on the central tank area which becomes a little cramped. The Bachmann tanks were cut in two and fixed slightly closer together. The outer ends were also shaved of 2mm and the box shapes reinstated with plastic card. Lead shot filled the compartments before lids were cut and fixed firmly in place.

RIGHT: Because of these adjustments, the footsteps no longer align with the engine room access door. Some new steps, assembled from plastic strip, try and disguise this anomaly.

BELOW: The success of the finished locomotive is open to debate but it does fulfil the main criteria set out by myself: it makes good use of an existing model and spare components, it brings an old model up to date and it doesn't immediately look out of place alongside my other Vi-Trains and Bachmann 37s.

I have to admit that there are some parts of this 'hybrid' model that I'd change if repeating the exercise but, overall, I think the time was well spent.

WHERE NEXT?

I still enjoy having a 'root' through bargain bins at exhibitions and swapmeets, looking for something that can plant a seed of inspiration in my mind: a thought of 'I could do something with that'. Unfortunately, it seems that some traders try and pass off what most people would term as 'junk' as 'collectables' and price it accordingly, so it pays to be discerning. We discussed new motors in Chapter 15, so finding a 'good runner' is not essential.

An alternative to the second-hand market is the new entry-level model range offered by Hornby under the Railroad banner that currently includes a number of senior product lines 'cascaded' from the main catalogue, such as the original tooling for the HST power car (supplied in pairs), the Class 47 and a reappearance of the former Lima Class 37. The low cost of these products and the quality mechanisms fitted are proving attractive to a market outside of the 'trainset' operator. Additionally, a small 0-6-0 diesel shunter is offered by Bachmann in its own Junior product line and this offers many freelance or industrial possibilities.

The term 'freelance' refers to models either drawn entirely from the imagination or based loosely on real prototypes but adapted to other periods, conditions or locations. An image is included overleaf as an example of a small shunting locomotive at work in the desert sands of Egypt and, although nothing such as this existed in reality, the US Army commissioned some vaguely similar machines for use during the Second World War. Why did I build this model? Well, it uses as its basis my first locomotive, taken from a Lima trainset marketed in the early 1980s for the British OO-gauge market and, despite the BR logos and running numbers, the loco was of Continental outline. The same mix of sentimentality and modelling opportunism were behind the conversion to a 'freelance' War Department engine.

The potential of using older models, or those in 'junior' ranges, is displayed here. Based on an old Lima 0-4-0 loco, supplied in trainsets during the 1980s (indeed, this one was from my first train set), the model has been substantially altered and re-powered to form a 'freelance' wartime machine based loosely on a US-built prototype in use in the Middle East.

Returning to the theme of entry-level models, perhaps the product with the most potential is the Railroad Class 06 0-4-0 shunting locomotive that will permit recreation of a bona fide BR machine. Although the model, as supplied, is inaccurate and a little coarse in detail, the addition of a bespoke re-motoring and super-detailing kit from Branchlines, makes for an enjoyable, if advanced, project; all for a similar price as most r-t-r locomotives. A less demanding route would be to aim for a fictional, industrial-style machine. By retaining the existing mechanism but enhancing the bodyshell, a convincing model could be produced.

Don't ever let it be said that the modern railway hobbyist now has little to do in terms of practical undertakings, despite the rise in quality of r-t-r stock. There will always be plenty of potential projects, only now we have a head start with high-quality models to use as a basis. The cost of new stuff is rising but, again, this offers its own opportunities in maximizing the potential of second-hand or older models. With a bank of techniques and a little confidence, only your imagination can hold you back. As I've heard my boss, Chris Leigh, say a number of times, there is a difference between 'railway modelling' and 'model railways'. Let's keep on with the modelling and keep our hobby alive.

Hornby's 'Railroad' range of entry level locomotives and rolling stock provides plenty of opportunities for the eager modeller.

Appendix: Useful Addresses

Trade

The Airbrush Company Ltd
Unit 7 Marlborough Road
Lancing Business Park
Lancing
West Sussex
BN15 8UF
Tel: 08700 660 445
www.airbrushes.com
Lifecolor paints, Iwata airbrushes, painting
equipment, Expo Tools and much more.

Alexander Models
37 Glanton Road
North Shields
Tyne & Wear
NE29 8LJ
Tel: 0191 257 6716
Email: alexandermodels@fsmail.net
Kits and components.

Axminster Power Tool Centre Ltd
Unit 10 Weycroft Avenue
Axminster
Devon
EX13 5PH
www.axminster.co.uk
Craft and hobby tools.

Branchlines
PO Box 4293
Westbury
BA13 9AA
Tel: 01373 822231
Email: sales@branchlines.com
Motors, gears, wheels and accessories.

Brassmasters
PO Box 1137
Sutton Coldfield
West Midlands
B76 1FU
www.brassmasters.co.uk
Kits and detailing components.

Aidan Campbell
22 Queens Road
Hoylake
Wirral
CH47 2AH
www.aidan-campbell.co.uk
OO-gauge figures.

Cammett Ltd
Unit 5, Greenfield Industrial Estate
Forest Road,
Hay-on-Wye
HR3 5FA
Tel: 01497 822757
www.cammett.co.uk
Modelling tools (including 'Hold 'n' Fold' and
'Nutter'), accessories and materials.

Crafty Computer Paper
Woodhall
Barrasford
Hexham
Northumberland
NE48 4DB
Tel: 01434 689 153
www.craftycomputerpaper.co.uk
Materials for DIY waterslide transfers.

Dart Castings
17 Hurst Close
Staplehurst
Tonbridge
Kent
TN12 0BX
www.dartcastings.co.uk
Cast figures suitable for early BR-era
locomotives.

DC Kits
111 Norwood Crescent
Staningley
Leeds
West Yorkshire
LS28 6NG
Tel: 0113 2563415
www.dckits.co.uk
R-t-r models, kits, components, accessories,
motor bogies, books and DVDs.

Deluxe Materials
Unit 13 Cufaude Business Park
Bramley
Hampshire
RG26 5DL
Tel: 01529 455 034
www.deluxematerials.com
Adhesives, fillers, applicators and scenics.

East Kent Models
89 High Street
Whitstable
Kent
CT5 1AY
Tel: 01227 770777
Hornby and Lima spare parts.

Express Models
65 Conway Drive
Shepshed
Loughborough
Leicestershire
LE12 9PP
Tel: 01509 829008
www.expressmodels.co.uk
Lighting units for locomotives, rolling stock
and layouts.

First Class Trains
221 Galmington Road
Taunton
Somerset
TA1 4ST
Tel: 01823 337460
Lighting units for locomotives.

Fox Transfers
4 Hill Lane Close
Markfield Industrial Estate
Markfield
Leicestershire
LE67 9PN
Tel: 01530 242801
www.fox-transfers.co.uk
Transfers, etched plates and paints.

Alan Gibson
(Workshop)
PO Box 597
Oldham
Lancashire
OL1 9FQ
Tel: 0161 678 1607
Detailing components, wheels and handrail
wire.

Hattons of Liverpool
364–368 Smithdown Road
Liverpool
L15 5AN
Tel: 0151 733 3655
www.hattons.co.uk
R-t-r models at discount prices.

Howes Models Ltd
12 Banbury Road
Kidlington
Oxon
OX5 2BT
Tel: 01865 848000
www.howesmodels.co.uk
R-t-r models, A1, Shawplan, Craftsman
Models, detailing components, Railmatch
paints and Heljan spare parts.

Hurst Models
PO Box 158
Newton-le-Willows
Warrington
WA12 0WW
www.hurstmodels.com
Kits, components and transfers.

Inter City Models
9–10 Celtic House
Harbour Head
Porthleven
Cornwall
TR13 9JY
Tel: 01326 569200
www.intercitymodels.com
Kits, components and source for Model Torque
motors.

Keen Systems
16 Elm Drive
Market Drayton
Shropshire
TF9 3HE
Tel: 01630 657881
www.keen-systems.com
Close coupling systems and detailing
accessories.

Mainly Trains
Unit C, South Road Workshops
Watchet
Somerset
TA23 0HF
Tel: 01984 634543
www.mainlytrains.co.uk
Tools (including Bill Bedford handrail bending
jig), materials, paints and own range of
detailing components.

MG Sharp Models
712 Attercliffe Road
Sheffield
South Yorkshire
S9 3RP
Tel: 0114 244 0851
www.mgsharp.com
R-t-r models, A1 Models detailing components
and Kadee couplings.

Modelmaster Decals
31 Crown Street
Ayr
KA8 8AG
Scotland
Tel: 01292 289770
www.modelmasterdecals.com
Transfers and etched plates.

Motorbogies.com
www.motorbogies.com
Custom-built or ready made re-motoring
solutions, including Black Beetle and BullAnt
motor units.

Phoenix Precision Paints
PO Box 8238
Chelmsford
Essex
CM1 7WY
Tel: 01245 494 050
www.phoenix-paints.co.uk
Paints, varnishes and thinners.

Precision Labels
www.precisionlabels.com
Also available from Frizinghall Models, tel:
01274 747447
Transfers and headcode panels.

Shawplan Model Products
2 Upper Dunstead Road
Langley Mill
Notts
NG16 4GR
Tel: 01773 718648
www.shawplan.com
Detailing components and nameplates.

Squires Model and Craft Tools
100 London Road
Bognor Regis
West Sussex
PO21 1DD
Tel: 01243 842424
www.squires.com
Tools, equipment and materials.

Ten Commandments
20 Struan Drive
Inverkeithing
Fife
KY11 1AR
www.cast-in-stone.co.uk
Printed detailing packs.

Ultrascale UK
Gear Services (Letchworth) Ltd
Unit 25 Such Close 2 Industrial Estate
Letchworth Garden City
Hertfordshire
SG6 1JF
Tel: 01462 681007
www.ultrascale.co.uk
Wheels, axles, motors and gears.

Wizard Models
PO Box 70
Barton upon Humber
DN18 5XY
Tel: 01652 635885
www.wizardmodels.co.uk
www.51l.co.uk
Spratt & Winkle couplings and detailing
components.

Manufacturers
Bachmann Europe plc
Moat Way
Barwell
Leics
LE9 8EY
Tel: 0870 751 9990
www.bachmann.co.uk

Hornby Hobbies Ltd
Westwood
Margate
Kent
CT9 4JX
www.hornby.com

Heljan UK
UK distributor:
Howes Models Ltd
12 Banbury Road
Kidlington
Oxon
OX5 2BT
Tel: 01865 848000
www.heljan.dk

Vi-Trains
UK distributor:
The Hobby Company
Garforth Place
Knowhill
Milton Keynes
MK5 8PG
Email: enquiries@hobbyco.net

Sources of Information
Diesel and Electric Modellers United (DEMU)
Membership Secretary
5 Selborne Close
Beaconhill Green
Cramlington
Northumberland
NE23 8HL
www.demu.co.uk

National Model Railroad Association (British
Region)
www.nmrabr.org.uk

UK Model Shop Directory
www.ukmodelshops.co.uk

Reference Material Sources
Bauer Consumer Media
Bushfield House
Orton Centre
Peterborough
PE2 5UW
Tel: 01733 288163
www.model-rail.com

Publishers of:
Model Rail
Four-weekly magazine covering all aspects of railway modelling, including all eras and worldwide subjects.
Rail
Fortnightly news magazine covering the contemporary British railway scene.

Foursight Publications Ltd
20 Park Street
Kings Cliffe
Peterborough
PE8 6XN
Tel: 01780 470 086
www.railexpress.co.uk
Publishers of:
Rail Express
Monthly magazine containing a modelling supplement concentrating solely on the diesel and electric era.

Freightmaster Publishing
Tel: 01793 644957
www.freightmasterpublishing.co.uk
Publishers of up-to-date British freight train timetables.

Ian Allan Publishing Ltd
Hersham
Surrey
KT12 4RG
www.ianallan.co.uk
Publishers of:
Hornby Magazine
Monthly railway modelling magazine, favouring the early BR period.
www.hornbymagazine.com
Railways Illustrated
Combining contemporary and heritage themes and news, published monthly.
www.railwaysillustrated.com
Also publishers of countless books on railway and transport history.

Midland Counties Publications
4 Watling Drive
Hinckley
LE10 3EY
Tel: 01455 233747
www.midlandcountiessuperstore.com
Publishers of an extensive range of railway-related titles.

Peco Publications and Publicity Ltd
Beer
Seaton
Devon
EX12 3NA
Tel: 01297 20580
www.peco-uk.com
Publishers of:
Railway Modeller
A long-standing monthly magazine dealing with all aspects of British-based railway modelling.

Platform 5 Publishing Ltd
3 Wyvern House
Sark Road
Sheffield
S2 4HG
Tel: 0114 255 8000
Publishers of annual volumes of locomotive and rolling stock registers.

The Railway Centre.com Ltd
PO Box 45
Dawlish
Devon
EX7 9XY
www.modern-locoillustrated.com
Publishers of:
Modern Locomotives Illustrated
Bi-monthly part-work magazine that covers, in depth, a particular post-steam locomotive class per issue.

Warners Group Publications plc
The Maltings
West Street
Bourne
Lincs
PE10 9PH
Publishers of:
Traction
Nostalgic, monthly magazine concentrating on diesel and electric subjects. Currently also includes a small D&E era modelling supplement.
www.traction.co.uk
British Railway Modelling
Monthly modelling magazine covering all aspects of the hobby.
www.britishrailwaymodelling.co.uk

Wild Swan Publications Ltd
1-3 Hagbourne Road
Didcot
Oxon
OX11 8DP
Tel: 01235 816 478
Publishers of:
Model Railway Journal
Bi-monthly journal aimed at the finescale modeller (mainly British-outline), across all periods. Also publishers of a range of books, concerning both the 'real' railways and railway modelling.

Bibliography

Books

Brewster, R., *The Art of Soldering* (Bernard Baboni, 1992)

Cain, T., *Soldering and Brazing* (Argus Books, 1985)

Clarke, D., *Diesels in Depth: Classes 24/25* (Ian Allan, 2006)

Clarke, D., *Diesels in Depth: Class 40* (Ian Allan, 2006)

Clough, D.N., *Locomotive Profile: Type 5 Freight Diesels* (Ian Allan, 1990)

Dunn, P. and Loader, M., *Class 20 Photo File* (Vanguard Publications, 2003)

Greaves, S., *Locomotive Datafile* (Metro Enterprises, 1988)

Lessard, M., *Airbrush Painting Techniques* (Osprey Publishing, 1999)

Longhurst, R., *Electric Locomotives on the West Coast Main Line* (Bradford Barton, 1980)

Lovett, D. and Wood, L. (Cade, R. and Gallafent, B., eds), *Cade's Locomotive Guide* (Marwain Publishing, 2007)

Marsden, C.J., *The AC Electrics* (OPC, 2007)

Marsden. C.J. and Fenn, G.B., *British Rail Mainline Electric Locomotives* (OPC, 1993)

Marsden. C.J., *The Complete BR Diesel and Electric Locomotive Directory* (OPC, 1991)

Marsden. C.J., *The Diesel Shunter: A Pictorial Record* (OPC, 1981)

Marsden. C.J., *The Power of the HSTs* (OPC, 2006)

Montague, K., *The Power of the Peaks* (OPC, 1978)

Morrison, G., *The Heyday of the Class 40s* (Ian Allan, 2005)

Morrison, G., *The Heyday of the Peaks* (Ian Allan, 2005)

Noble, T., *Profile of the Class 26s and 27s* (OPC, 1982)

Nicolle, B.J., *Modern Diesels in Focus* (Ian Allan, 1979)

Shannon, P., *Blue Diesel Days* (Ian Allan, 2007)

Tayler, A.T.H., Thorley, W.G.F. and Hill, T.J., *Class 47 Diesels* (Ian Allan, 1979)

Toms, G., *Brush Diesel Locomotives* 1940–78 (Turntable Transport Publishing, 1978)

Vaughan, J., *Class 40s at Work* (Ian Allan, 1981)

Vaughan, J., *Diesels on the London Midland* (Ian Allan, 1981)

Webb, B., *English Electric Mainline Diesels of British Railways* (David and Charles, 1976)

Welch, M., *The Art of Weathering* (Wild Swan, 1993)

Articles

Bayer, G., 'Ten Steps to Obtaining 'Peak' Perfection', *Rail Express Modeller* (July 2004, pp.50–51)

Bendall, S., 'Class 40s: Whistling Giants', *Rail Express Modeller* (December 2005, pp.XX–XXIII)

Bendall, S., 'Evolution not Revolution: Class 25 Masterclass', *Model Rail* (July 2002, pp.18–26)

Bendall, S., 'Old Faithful 08', *Model Rail* (June 2001, pp.20–30)

Clinnick, R., 'Roaring 20s', *Rail* (Issue 563, April 11–April 24 2007, pp.56–59)

Davies, J., 'The Class 20s Today', *Railway Modeller* (May 1988, pp.230–233)

Dunn, P., 'A Locomotive for All Duties: Class 37/4 Masterclass', *Model Rail* (Autumn 1998, pp.18–27)

Dunn, P., 'A Touch of Class 26 in Scotland', *Model Rail* (July 2000, pp.20–28)

Gilson, C., 'Turning Up the Heat' (Class 37 refurbishment), *Rail* (Issue 529, December 21 2005–January 3 2006, pp.56–57)

Johnson, P., 'Hybrid 'Rat' Combines the Best of Both Worlds', *Rail Express* Modeller (November 2004, pp.XVI–XVII)

INDEX

A1 Models
  buffers 66–67, 106, 154
  Class 37 body side grille pack 178
  Class 44 heavy duty grille pack 146–148
  Class 58 detailing parts 84–86
  exhaust grilles 146
  interior pipe-work 49–50
  multiple working mounts 104
  radio roof pod 156
  snowploughs 68, 86–88
  window surrounds for DRS Class 20 156
  WIPAC light clusters 156
  wipers 30
abrasives
  scratch brush 33, 86
  paper 52, 77, 79, 86, 114, 118, 139, 145, 147, 154, 156
  wire wool 52, 118
adhesives
  accelerants 25, 106
  cyanoacrylate (superglue) 25, 29, 33, 41
  epoxy 25–26, 96, 98, 112, 144, 163, 170
  Glue 'n' Glaze 81–82, 103
  gluing 29, 31–35, 170
  Loctite thread sealant 68
  odourless cyanoacrylate 25, 31, 82
  Pin Flow glue applicator 26, 102, 154
  plastic cement 26, 102, 154, 176
  PVA 26, 48
  Super Crylic 26
  Tacky Glue 26, 58
  Tacky Wax 41, 44
aerosol
  airbrush cleaners 125
  paint 123
  primers 119
  propellant 126
Airbrush
  airbrushes 124–126
  air supplies 126
  health and safety 124
  weathering 132–133, 137
The Airbrush Company 120, 125, 131
Alexander Models 179
Automatic Warning System (AWS) 47, 115
Bachmann
  CIE GM Class 141/181 9
  Class 04 49, 69–71
  Class 08 110–111, 137
  Class 20 41, 88, 95, 133, 137, 156–157
  Class 24 47
  Class 25 47, 145–146
  Class 37 11, 31, 57–58, 74–76, 125, 145, 173, 175–180
  Class 40 41, 134–135
  Class 44 146–148
  Class 45 110
  Class 46 34, 140–141
  Class 47 58–59, 138–139
  Class 55 64–65
  Class 57 36–36
  'Deltic' prototype 10, 27
  Class 66 67, 93–94
  Junior range 181
Black Beetle 162–163, 165
boiler
  compartment 145, 178

exhaust port 23, 154, 145–146, 178
  water tanks 111, 117
bogies
  enhancing 86, 105–106, 142, 154–155, 157
  footsteps 105, 108, 142, 179
  modifying 142, 150–152, 157, 179
  sanding pipes 103, 106
  springs 150–151
brakes
  air brake equipment 114–115, 117
  disc insert 159
  pipes 28–29
  shoes 179
branchlines 164–165, 182
brass
  castings 106–107
  cutting 30, 32–34
  etched components 22, 24, 30, 32–34, 41, 74–76, 84–88, 103–104, 142–144, 146–149, 154–157, 177–178
  folding 20, 71–73, 85, 87, 144
  gluing 30, 32–34, 144
  rolling 74–75, 84
  sheet 22–23
  soldering 18, 86–88, 105, 162
  strip 22–23, 73, 103–105, 111, 163
  wire 22–23, 35, 70–73, 86–87, 102, 110, 143, 156–157, 178–179
British Railways/British Rail/BR 8, 32, 37–38, 42–43, 69, 76, 124, 174, 181
buffers
  back plates 67, 88, 154
  bufferbeams 15–16, 26–29, 178
  fitting replacements 66–68, 154
  removal 66–67, 101
  steps 67, 154
BullAnt 163–165
cantrail warning stripes 127–128
Carrs Metal Black solution 166
Class 04
  building an interior 48–49
  fitting handrails 69–70
  glazing 82
  jackshaft mesh cover 71
Class 08
  adding a driver 42
  enhancing cab interior 47
  extra underframe piping 110–111
  fitting brake pipes 28–29
  weathering 137
Class 20
  adding lamp brackets 88
  DRS conversion 156–157
  etched headcode discs 88
  fitting Kadee couplings 91–92
  masked for warning panels 121
  new buffers 88
  speedometer 157
  weathering 133, 137
  wire handrails 88
Class 24
  headcode discs 37–40
  interior 47
Class 25
  blanking-off boiler grille 145–146
  enhancing cab interiors 47
  original exhaust port conversion 145–146
  painting 120, 127
Class 26
  correcting nose detail 141–142
  underframe air tanks 117

Class 27
  blending new paint 126–127
  bufferbeam detail 26
  changing overhead warning flashes 54, 65
  prototype details 15–16
Class 31
  fitting etched headcode discs 41
  heavily weathered prototype 129
Class 33
  applying yellow warning panel 121
  of headcode 60
Class 37
  air horns 31–32, 149, 178
  buffers 66–68
  bogie footsteps 142, 179
  bogie frame replacement 179
  CP7 bogie modification 141–142
  livery amendments 75, 125
  nameplates 34
  rebuilding a Hornby Class 37 174–181
  rebuilt front ends 149–150
  re-numbering by patch-painting 62–63
  snowploughs 68–69, 86–88
  Western Region lamp brackets 75
  windscreen surrounds 143–144
  wipers 25
Class 40
  engine room window pipework 50
  faded paintwork 135
  interior detail (real 47
  weathering 134–136
Class 43 (HST)
  fitting Keen Systems couplings 97–99
  underframe detail 117
Class 44
  conversion to heavy duty grille arrangement 146–148
Class 45
  underframe details 109–110
Class 46
  fitting etched nameplates 34
  nose seam line 140–141
Class 47
  bogie detail correction 139
  cantrail warning stripe 127–128
  changing back-lit headcodes 58–59
  correcting windscreens 138
  DRS conversion 153–155
  engine room window pipework 49–50
  fitting working lights 170–172
  Flushglazing 81
  prototype detail 14
  re-numbering 53–56
  replacing moulded handrails 77–78
  speedometer 155
  underframe details 111–112
  weathering 132–133
  wipers 30–31
Class 50
  interior detail (real) 46
Class 55
  re-naming 64–65
  varnishing 65
Class 56
  cab interiors 43–45
  comparison with older model 9
  fitting scale couplings 94–95
  weathering with Tamiya pigments 131–132

Class 57
  enhancing Delner coupling 35–36
Class 58
  adding etched brass grilles 84–86
  cleaning glazing 80
  removing moulded grilles 83–84
Class 60
  distressing bodywork 135
  re-numbering 54
  weathering 135–136
Class 66
  fitting Kadee couplings 93–94
  fitting sprung buffers 67
  rear view mirrors 72–73
Class 67
  brake disc overlays 159
  cab interior 46
  fitting working lights 167–169
  re-numbering 56, 61–62
  underframe details 113–115
  weathering 133
Class 73
  underframe details 115–117
Class 86
  bogie conversion 150–152
  multiple working fittings 152
  new pantograph 152
  superdetailing 150–152
Class 87
  extra power collection 162
  guttering 102
  multiple working equipment 102
  re-motoring 160–162, 164
  re-wheeling 161, 164
  roof top details 101, 104
  sanding pipes 103
Class 91
  bogie footsteps 105
  bufferbeam detail 106
  new pantograph 106–107
  rooftop detail 107
  sanding pipes 106
  valances 106
  wheels 159
Class 92
  cab interior sun blinds 48
  fitting Channel Tunnel logos 32–33
  re-wheeling 164–166
copper
  copper-clad board 162
  wire 22, 162
couplings
  compatibility 89–90
  cosmetic 94
  Delner coupling 35–36
  Eazi-Mate 94
  Kadee 91–94, 97, 100
  Keen system 96–98
  Roco 90
  scale couplings 94–95, 99
  Spratt & Winkle 99–100
  tension lock 89–90
  NEM 90–93, 95, 97
Craftsman Models
  bogie footsteps 142, 179
  cab window overlays 143, 178
  jumper cables 106
  wipers 30
decals
  application 55–56
  colour patches 56
  DIY transfers 64
  preparation 53, 56
  softening solution 56, 61–62
  types and brands 53–54, 56, 154–155
  varnishing 55, 62, 64–65

Diesel & Electric Modellers United (DEMU) 12
digital command control 11
DC Kits 101, 107, 152, 163
DRS 48, 104, 153–157
EWS 43, 56, 61, 71, 73, 142
figures 42–45, 49
fishing wire 24, 103
footsteps 15, 105, 108, 142, 179
Fox Transfers
  nameplates 33–34
  transfers 53–54, 56, 154
freelance modelling 181–182
Freightliner 39, 43, 152
fuel
  drains 109–111
  fillers 16, 110
  spillage 129, 137
  tanks 16, 109, 111–117, 156–157, 180
glazing
  DIY plastic 82
  Flushglaze 81, 152
  Glue 'n' Glaze liquid glazing 81–82, 103
  removal 168
  repairing 80
GNER 104
grilles
  fitting etched replacements 74–75, 84–86, 146–148, 178
  removing mouldings 83–84, 146–147
guitar strings 24
handrails
  knobs 69–70
  plastic 22, 69, 77–78, 101
  replacing 69–72, 77–78, 85–86, 88
  wire 24, 69–73, 78
headcodes
  alpha-numerical 57–60
  discs 37–41, 148
head lights
  drilling-out moulded lights 103
  high intensity 150, 156
  round, with rubber grommet 102
Heljan
  Class 26 26, 117, 140–141
  Class 27 26, 58, 65, 126–127
  Class 33 26, 68, 106
  Class 47 51, 53–54
  Class 57 35
  Class 58 83, 85
  printed headcodes 58, 60
  snowploughs 68
  spare parts 30, 45, 68, 111–112, 154–155
high visibility clothing 43, 45–46, 155
Hobbycraft 35
Hornby
  Class 08 28, 42
  Class 31 41–42
  Class 35 77
  Class 37 173–181
  Class 43 (HST) 99, 181
  Class 47 45, 111, 173, 181
  Class 50 77
  Class 56 9, 42, 44–45, 77, 95, 131–132, 167
  Class 58 80, 83–86
  Class 59 77
  Class 60 8, 42, 53–54, 135–136
  Class 66 77
  Class 67 46, 56, 61–62, 113–115, 133, 168–169
  Class 73 77, 80, 115–116
  Class 86 77, 101
  Class 90 101

Class 91 101, 104–108
Class 92 8, 32–33, 101, 165–167
Dublo 90
  motors 105, 158–160
  Rail Road range 181–182
  spare parts 45
  supplied detailing parts 28–29
  wheels 158–159, 164–166
horns
  improving mouldings 31
  replacement 31–32, 149
Hurst Models
  Channel Tunnel logos 32
  Class 47 engine room pipework 49–50
  pantograph 106–107
interiors
  bulkheads 46–47
  cab s 42-49
  colour schemes 46–47
  control desks 42, 45, 49
  engine room equipment 49–50
  sun blinds 48
lamps
  brackets 76, 88
  oil lamps 37
lead shot 110–111, 115–116, 180
LEDs 167, 170
lighting
  Light Store units 167–169
  working model lights 167–172
  workspace lighting 21
Lima
  Class 37 174, 181
  Class 43 (HST) 97–99, 167
  Class 47 10, 31, 50, 77–78, 109, 111–112, 153–155, 170–172
  Class 67 109, 168
  Class 73 109
  Class 87 101–104
  extra power collection 162
  freelance 0-4-0 shunter 163, 181–182
  re-wheeling 161
mainline
  blue (livery) 62–63
  Class 03 69
Mainly Trains
  cosmetic drawhooks 96
  etched chequer plate 67
  etched handwheels 110
  etched rivet strip 149, 157
  handrail bending jig 73
  strip brass 73, 105
masking
  masking tape & film 35, 61, 75, 120–121, 177
  masking fluid 61, 65, 120–121
  masking-up 61–65, 119–121, 126–127
methylated spirit 52, 56
Milliput 45, 79, 114
model filler 31, 79, 107, 113–114, 144, 149, 151, 156–157, 176, 178–179
ModelTorque 160–162
Modernization Plan 8
motors
  maintenance 158–159
  motor bogies 162–164
  re-motoring 159–162
  spare parts 159
  upgrading 159, 179
Murphy's Models 9
nameplates
  changing 63–64
  etched 32–34, 63–64
  fitting 33–34, 64
  printed 34, 63–64
  removal 34, 63–64
National Railway Museum 10, 14

nickel silver
  components 22, 24
  cutting 32–34
  wire 103–104, 151–152, 155
Nitromors 128
NMRA 165
paint
  acrylic 30, 123, 126
  bow pen 127–128
  brushes 124
  cellulose 123
  Cherry Paints 123
  cleaning 125
  enamels 30, 122–123, 126
  figures 43–45
  Humbrol 61, 71, 73, 122–124
  Lifecolor 122–123, 127
  mixing 126
  new parts 30, 35, 41, 71, 73, 76, 104, 111
  patch-painting 34, 62–63, 78
  Phoenix Precision Paint 122, 154
  preparation 30, 118–119
  primer 119, 179
  Railmatch 61, 63, 73, 122–123, 154
  spraying 64–65
  stripping 128
  thinner/thinning 122, 126
  varnish/varnishing 62, 64–65, 123–124
pantograph
  construction 106–107
  fitting 107, 152
  types 101, 104
plastic
  adhesives for 25–26
  plastic card 22, 112–114, 145, 156–157
  rod, strip & section 22, 49, 103, 110–117, 139, 143, 148–149, 151–152, 154–157, 176, 178
  types of 21–22
re-numbering 51–56, 61–62
resin 24
Royal Train 40
safety 18–24, 124, 128
sanding pipes 103, 106, 143
scratch-building
  detailing components 102–106, 143, 148, 151–152, 154–157
  interiors 48–49
  underframe components 105–106, 113–115, 151, 155, 157, 180
Shawplan
  buffer back plates 154
  buffers 66
  Channel Tunnel logos 32–33
  coach fittings 177
  headcode discs 41
  headcode panels 149, 178
  lamp brackets 76
  nameplates 33
  radiator fans and grilles 74–75
  roof top fire extinguishers 104
  snowploughs 68
  WIPAC light clusters 156
  wipers 30
snow ploughs
  etched brass 68, 87–88, 175
  fitting 68–69, 87–88
  headcode disc display for snowplough duty 37
  moulded plastic 68–69
soldering
  clamping 87
  flux 18, 87
  solder 18, 86–87
  soldering 86–88, 105, 162, 169–171

surface preparation 86
irons & tools 18
stainless steel
  mesh 71
  nameplates 33
  wheel inserts 159
T-Cut 33, 52–56, 58, 61–62, 65, 76
tools
  callipers 19
  cutting & filing 19, 22, 107, 138–139, 140, 146–147, 176–177
  drilling 26, 29, 30–31, 35, 49, 66–67, 69, 72, 78, 83, 95, 98, 102, 110, 139, 143, 146–147, 149, 154, 163, 168, 170, 178
  drills 20, 80, 113–114
  holding 20–21, 140
  Hold 'n' Fold 21, 85, 88
  measuring & marking 19–20
  'Nutter' 21
  pliers 17
  scriber & scribing 19, 140–141, 177
  tweezers 17
TOPS 53, 55, 154, 174
Tri-ang 89–90
underframe
  components 16, 109–117, 179–180
  detailing & modifying 109–117, 151, 155, 157, 179–180
  material 21–22
Virgin Trains 35, 150
Vi-Trains
  Class 37 25, 27, 30, 34, 52, 62–63, 66, 69, 88, 141–144, 149–150, 180
  re-numbering method 62–63
  supplied parts 69
warning panel
  modifying 76, 78, 125
  masking-up 120–121
  cleaning seeped paint under masking 127
weathering
  considerations 130–131
  distressing 135
  dry-brushing 136
  faded paint 135, 137
  Humbrol 134, 136
  masking windows 133
  Metal Cote 134
  powders 131–132
  Railmatch weathering shades 132–133, 137
  spraying 132–133, 135
  talcum powder 137
  Tamiya pigments 131–132, 136
  Tensocrom paints 136–137, 148
wheels
  back-to-back gauge 166
  cleaning 158
  dismantling 160–161, 166
  fixing to axles 166
  profile 165
  replacing 161, 164–166
  ultrascale 159, 161, 165–166, 179
white-metal
  castings 22, 49, 106, 178
  working with 22, 49, 106
white spirit 52, 56, 118
windscreens
  etched windscreen surrounds 156, 143, 178
  creating 'wiped' windscreens when weathering 133
  washer jets 157
  wipers 25, 30–31
WIPAC light clusters 153, 156